Mentoring with a Humane Face

Third Edition

Dr. Narayan Persaud

CENGAGE Learning™

Australia • Brazil • Japan • Korea • Mexico • Singapore • Spain • United Kingdom • United States

CENGAGE
Learning™

Mentoring with a Humane Face: Third Edition

Dr. Narayan Persaud

Executive Editors:
Michele Baird
Maureen Staudt
Michael Stranz

Project Development Manager:
Linda deStefano

Senior Marketing Coordinators:
Sara Mercurio
Lindsay Shapiro

Production/Manufacturing Manager:
Donna M. Brown

PreMedia Services Supervisor:
Rebecca A. Walker

Rights & Permissions Specialist:
Kalina Hintz

Cover Image:
Getty Images*

* Unless otherwise noted, all cover images used by Custom Solutions, a part of Cengage Learning, have been supplied courtesy of Getty Images with the exception of the Earthview cover image, which has been supplied by the National Aeronautics and Space Administration (NASA).

ISBN-13: 978-0-7593-8904-5

ISBN-10: 0-7593-8904-7

Cengage Learning
5191 Natorp Boulevard
Mason, Ohio 45040
USA

Cengage Learning is a leading provider of customized learning solutions with office locations around the globe, including Singapore, the United Kingdom, Australia, Mexico, Brazil, and Japan. Locate your local office at: **international.cengage.com/region**

Cengage Learning products are represented in Canada by Nelson Education, Ltd.

For your lifelong learning solutions, visit **custom.cengage.com**

Visit our corporate website at **cengage.com**

Printed in the United States of America

Dedication

To my wife **Pabitri,** my sons **Shiv** and **Shashi** all of whom showed me endless love. And to the hundreds of mentors who served with me in the community and schools.

ACKNOWLEDGEMENTS

This supplement is the outgrowth of over ten years of mentoring at-risk African American youths that involved the painstaking efforts of a host of individuals. To all of them I owe my sincere thanks. To the late Judge Charles Miner Jr., the architect of the Juvenile Justice Role Model Development Program (JJRMDP), a jurist who has never flinched in his efforts to assist at-risk youths. May his Soul rest in peace with the thought that his commitment to save at-risk youths lives on.

Over the years, several of my colleagues at Florida Agricultural and Mechanical University (FAMU) supported my mentoring efforts, Owusu Agyapong, Melvin Barber, Emit Hunt, Felicia Dix-Richardson, Olugbemi Moloye and Jackie Perkins. Olu and Jackie spent many hours listening to my stories regarding the plight of at-risk youth, and challenged me to develop a better understanding of the disadvantaged. Jackie enlightened me on what it means to be a single-parent and facilitated my efforts to involve parents in the mentoring process. To the hundreds of FAMU students who spent numberless hours mentoring, I am deeply indebted. It is indeed impossible to identify all of them by their names. Cory, Tanika, Danille, Toya, Kinetra, Willie, Monekka, Maurice, Danae and Chris, all spent numerous hours soliciting the support of other students in our mentoring efforts, and were very instrumental in building the Role Model Program. Several students are heard throughout these pages and to them I owe special thanks. And, to Speedy and Lance, who in their youth, gave me the opportunity to be a mentor.

Many parents, grandparents, great-grandparents and youths have helped to make this project possible. Their willingness to share their stories has served as my source of inspiration. I am truly thankful for their candidness and support to let their stories and lived circumstances be known. To Ms. Trudie Perkins who at age eighty-four still cares for, and mentors for her great- grandchild Tashi Martin. Ms. Perkins epitomizes the resiliency and centrality of the elderly female in the African American family.

I would also like to thank Carmen Cummings, who as one of the anchors of Channel 6 Television spent many hours with us in the field, visiting mentees, their parents and grandparents, and some times accompanying us to juvenile court. With Carmen's support we were able to bring into the public's view the plight of at-risk African American youths. Bill Berlow of the Tallahassee Democrat also encouraged and assisted me in bringing into public view, the plight of at-risk youths, and to him I am also grateful. I would also like to thank Andrea Walker who has assisted us in our efforts to reach out into the community. Over the years Andrea has become a close friend. Thanks also to Alice Simms who supported our mentoring efforts with great enthusiasm, and who provided internships to many of our mentors. Thanks to Ulyses Hooks, my graduate assistant for reading the manuscript and offering suggestions.

This project would not have come to fruition had it not been for the support and encouragement of Kristin Cunningham and Kathryn Warren of Thomson's Learning. Kristin's encouragement helped me to forge ahead with the project.

Special thanks to my sons Shiv and Shashi who taught me how to be a better father, and mentor. And, to my dear wife Pabitri who not only encouraged me to work on this project, but willingly pardoned my mood swings when my thinking became muddled and I became irritable. Finally, to my brother Lionel Shiv Persaud who showed me the way.

FOREWORD

If we live in a world where every child has a mentor, can you imagine what a world that would be? If we live in a world where the phrase, *No child shall be left behind,* is a sincere proposition and not merely a politician's campaign theme, can you imagine what a difference that would make? For many elderly African Americans such things were not left to the imagination, they were real.

As I look around the African American community, it seemed like not so long ago mothers, fathers, grandparents, uncles, aunts, sister, brothers, neighbors, friends, teachers and preachers were all role models and mentors. This was their way of life, fashioned from the depths of the struggles for survival. The older men and women of the African American community nurtured and cared for their own children, their neighbors' children, the community's children. Yes, children belonged to the community as a whole, and their role models and mentors were almost every adult member in the community.
Back then, no one referred to them as mentors, they were just the people who were a part of the village that helped to raise the child. Few children had to go outside of their homes or the community in search of a mentor. The world, however, is not the same, and we are not living in yesterday.

Today, societal changes have placed a growing number of African American youth at risk. It is out of the concern for the at-risk youth that the Juvenile Justice Role Model Development Program (JJRMDP) at Florida A&M University took birth in 1994. Designed to train and develop students to serve as mentors and role models for at-risk youth within the community, the Program has impacted the lives of many. In the pages that follow, you will hear some of the most poignant stories of many at-risk youths and their families as told by their mentors. Persaud, indeed, has skillfully pulled together a complex array of real life situations into a coherent analysis of the subtleties of mentoring.

Mentoring is not a one-time activity or a leisure class fancy. It is a personal commitment that requires honesty and dedication. The author of this text knows that first hand. Anyone who has followed Persaud into the communities and courtrooms, as I have, would realize his sincerity and indepth understanding of the plight of African American youth. He, like them, has had to deal with the harsh realities of poverty, discrimination, indifference and degradation.

I still remember vividly the countless hours Persaud and I spent in the Role Model house listening to the stories recounted by mentors. From their narrations, it became clear that many were unprepared to face the harsh realities of young children who bore the pains of deprivation in their small minds and bodies. I also remember the many times we went to juvenile court and took front row seats, only to hear of the horrors of poverty on the young as told by mothers and grandmothers, all searching for answers. As we watched mothers and grandmothers (some with curlers in their hair and bedroom slippers on their feet) plead and cried for their children and grandchildren, it seemed as if no one in authority cared. This led many mentors to ask if these happenings were "real." To such a question Persaud would invariably reply: "It is indeed real, just as you have witnessed."

On the whole, Persaud's book is not only easy to read, its' presentations are vivid, and the lessons offered are very valuable. Anyone seeking to undertake mentoring as a voluntary activity will most likely find the book a valuable resource.

Jacqueline Perkins
Director of Internships, FAMU

Contents

CHAPTER 1

The good looks beyond the external accidents and discerns those internal qualities that make all men human and, therefore brothers.

Martin Luther King Jr.

Introduction

Mentoring as a way to enhance young lives and ameliorate social problems of youth has become quite commonplace as government, public and private organizations form alliances to help mould the young into becoming successful adults. Promoted as an activity whereby individuals can "give back to their communities", mentoring seems to have permeated all sectors of society, bringing into closer contact with one another, the privileged and underprivileged, old and young, achievers and underachievers, college students and grade schoolers etc.

In recent years, the popularization and sometimes glamorization of mentoring through the print and visual media has ushered into many communities and schools a wide array of mentors, all eager to guide and assist economically disadvantaged youths cope with the vicissitudes of daily life. In the main, these volunteers cut across all cultural and socio-economic sectors of society. Motivated to serve by a host of reasons: (1) Some individuals elect to become mentors because of their desires to assist the disadvantaged; (2) Others choose it as a form of reciprocation for benefiting from the guidance and encouragement they received from someone; and (3) Many view mentoring as a way whereby they can utilize their lived experiences of poverty and deprivation to assist others who are suffering similar consequences. In sum, many people look upon mentoring as a way to give back to their communities. The cases of Mary, Cory and Monekka help to illustrate the varying reasons why some people choose mentoring as their form of volunteerism.

In this first example, Mary, an affable grandmother of seven explained that *her experiences growing up as a disadvantaged African American served as the catalyst for becoming a mentor.* Knowing that Mary constantly gives back to the African American community, I asked her if she could write a short summary about her motivation to serve the disadvantaged. "That would be bragging about the little I do, don't you think so?" she asked. This is Mary as I have come to know her over the years.

Mentoring as a Way of Life: Mary the Affable Grandmother:

Many people who know Mary, regularly describe her as the, "grandma with a big heart." Mary's generosity precedes her, even though she is not a high paid bureaucrat. "A few times when I was short of money to get some food for the children, Mary would be the first to empty her pocket-book to give," said Andrea, the director of the family center at a low income housing complex. One morning when I phoned Mary, I playfully asked, "Are you taking it easy today?"
"I am," Mary replied laughingly. "I am just preparing a little something for a friend from church whose daughter is graduating." I smiled to myself because I know that when Mary says, "preparing a little something," it means cooking to feed a house full of people.

Watching Mary work with at-risk youths, *one is amazed at her ability to grasp the immediate circumstances and utilize this understanding in her mentoring decisions. She would coax, cajole, discipline, and supervise their games with great enthusiasm, fairness and exuberance.* "I grew up in a home where disrespect, dishonesty and animosity were not tolerated. My parents were disciplinarians, not strict, but disciplinarians nonetheless," she said. "They bestowed on me much love and respect, and I loved and respected them in return. If I can do the same for these children, they would all benefit in some ways."

For Mary, growing up as a child had its hardships. "I am what you will call a *door-step-child*," Mary explained. "My mother literally left me at the door of a childless elderly couple who became my Godparents. My Godfather died when I was ten years old, but my Godmother took care of me as if I was her own. We had some hard times, yet my Godmother never complained. She was a loving, caring human being. Despite being poor, she insisted that I never stopped dreaming about a better future." Mary paused as tears welled up in her eyes. She seemed to have recalled the loving relationship she had with her Godparents.

Mary went on to explain that her Godmother was her source of inspiration. "She took me in a stranger and turned me into her own, with love. Oh! Lots of love, and endless devotion. If there is one thing she insisted on was to get an education. My Godmother felt so strongly about education she made sure that I focused on graduating from high school before having any type of serious boyfriend-girlfriend relationship."

When Mary finished high school, she found employment and worked for a while. She then attended Wayne State University, where she earned her Bachelors degree in Criminology. In her late twenties, she met her husband. They got married when she became thirty. Shortly after marriage, Mary and her husband moved to Tallahassee to be closer to his relatives. In Tallahassee, Mary quickly became involved in the church and community. At first, she and her husband struggled to make ends meet but their faith in each other and in the Supreme kept them together. "We've had some really hard times, but my husband and I were determined to make it," she said. After a few years of hardships, Mary's life began to change as she and her husband found better employment. While employed, Mary's yearning for advanced education never ceased. Balancing job, school and family, she successfully completed her Masters degree, without relinquishing her community service. During her years of graduate studies, Mary became active in the Juvenile Justice Role Model Development Program's mentoring efforts to assist at-risk youths.

On her first day in the field, Mary took charge of a group of rowdy youths who quickly succumbed to her admonition. She did so with such skill and affection that left several of the accompanying mentors in awe. Today, Mary has become a surrogate grandmother to a number of disadvantaged youths. On any given weekend, it is not unusual to find Mary in a shopping mall or supermarket surrounded by her grandchildren and other youngsters, all clamoring for her attention and asking almost at once, "Can I get this, can I get that?" Andrea sums up Mary's mentoring best when she said: "You may never see her face on the newspaper pages but you will always see her impressions on the hearts and minds of the youths she serves."

Recently, I saw Mary at a gas station. In her usual exuberance she greeted me and proudly explained that two of the youths she mentored over the years are now enrolled in college.

Unlike Mary, *some people become mentors because they have benefited from the guidance and support they received from other individuals who served as their mentors.* Such is the case of Corey. A mild mannered young man with a hearty laugh, Corey was a "star" defensive tackle on the university's football team. Daily, he worked diligently to master the game with the hope that he would be able to play professional football. Then, he got hurt. The injury he sustained ended his college football career and a chance of playing in the National Football League (NFL). As he was suffering in silence and unsure of his future, Corey developed a relationship with his professor who became his mentor. This is how Corey explained the changes in his life and how be benefited by having a mentor.

A Mentor's Mentor: Corey, the Mild Mannered Former College Defensive Tackle:

As far back as I can recall I always dreamed that one day I will be playing in the National Football league. After a successful stint in high school, I was recruited to play at Florida Agricultural and Mechanical University (FAMU). At FAMU, I quickly earned a starting position as a defensive tackle. I was thrilled. I was on my way to the NFL. I knew then that the road to professional football would be difficult so, I worked hard and gained the respect of my coaches. Then, in my senior year, I was injured. It happened so fast, I can hardly recall the events. My dream of becoming a professional football player ended abruptly. My make believe world came crashing down on me. I always had the athlete's mentality that becoming a professional player was my ultimate goal in life.

When the doctor told me I would not be able to play football again, I refused to accept that my football career was over. Immediately, I went into denial. As the days turned into weeks and my broken ankle still pained, I would lock myself in my room feeling depressed and sorry for myself. "What am I going to do now that my dreams are shattered?" I asked myself regularly. This drove me into deeper depression.

In the early stages of my injury, I continued to room with members of my football team. My teammates, my friends, and my coaches all visited and offered words of encouragement. But, as the weeks turned into months, the visits got less and less. Each day, I was driven deeper into depression. I would lie in bed and stare at the ceiling believing there was no hope in the future. Most days, I had to drag myself out of bed to go to my classes, and to my student-job at the Sociology and Criminal Justice Department. At the department, most professors would stop to chat for a few minutes, even before, and then after my injury.

One day, deep into my depression, Dr. P (not his real name) stopped by, "Core," he said, "I am sorry you no longer have a chance to play in the NFL, but have you thought of what you are going to do after graduation?" Since my entire life thus far was to dream of playing football, I never thought of an alternative career. So, when Dr. P asked the question, I thought it was sort of weird. Then, he asked, "Core, how would you like to help some poor at-risk youths?" Not to disappoint him, I reluctantly agreed. The next day, Dr. P and I were out visiting Jimmy (my first mentee), and other poor children and their families in low-income neighborhoods, listening to their problems and assigning them mentors. Some times we drove for miles through narrow country roads to visit a child. Some times we went to court to plead on behalf of delinquent youths. It didn't matter whether they were Caucasian or African American. I've seen the tears of many youths, their single-parent mothers, their elderly grandmothers, and these expressions of sadness literally tore my heart. "There are too many youngsters in need of help," my mind kept saying. It didn't take a week, and without realizing when it happened, my depression left and never returned.

From that time on Dr. P became my mentor, teaching me, and several other students, how to become mentors. **What I learned as a mentor is that a person never stops learning how to be a mentor**. Many nights after classes, and hours of mentoring, we would gather in Dr. P's office to share our thoughts and seek answers to the problems of youths. "You cannot mentor a child in isolation," Dr. P would regularly impress on us. "**When you become a mentor to an at-risk child, you can make a significant difference if you could tap into his or her inner thoughts, feelings and emotions, and make these yours to the extent that it is possible. This will enable you to see the things he or she sees, and feel the things he or she feels**." For me, these statements rang so true, it is hard to describe. In my depressed state, I didn't get the feeling that people understood my emotional state and what I was going through. Knowing I

> wouldn't be able to play professional football was like living in utter darkness, dazed and discarded. From the way people treated me, and then distanced themselves from me, I felt unwanted, I felt useless just like the many the poor children who are shunned or neglected by their parents, their teachers, their friends, even society.
>
> Having Dr. P. as my mentor brought me enormous satisfaction, and gave my life a new sense direction. Because of my mentoring work, I was featured as *The Person of the Week* by one of the local television stations. Today, I work with youths and am more passionate about mentoring because I know its' benefits. As I go about my mentoring each day, I always keep at the back of my mind that my life changed because someone took the time to be my mentor, (Mentor: Corey).

Corey made clear that mentoring is not a one shot affair, and that to be a successful mentor, one needs to be able to mentally place himself/herself in the situation of the mentee. These are important considerations and must be taken seriously by anyone undertaking the task of mentoring a child. Corey is now applying this lesson to his work with at-risk youths in Georgia, guiding them away from a life of delinquency and crime, and promoting the pursuit of education as a way to success.

For reasons that differ from that of Corey, *some individuals elect to become mentors because they understand the consequences of poverty and deprivation.* The belief is that the real life experiences can be shared to influence and turn around the lives of others, since the stories are actual real life accounts of the effects of poverty, and being disadvantaged. In the example that follows, Monekka explains the growing pains and difficulties she faced as an at-risk African American female. While serving as a mentor, Monekka drew constantly from her own past to connect with, and inspire her mentees. In presenting the reasons why she became a mentor, Monekka touched on several sensitive aspects of her life. Asked if some of the information in her essay should be deleted, *she explained that omitting a few painful incidents would not change or nullify her lived experiences.* Monekka hopes that in sharing her experiences truthfully, these will serve to inspire other disadvantaged females, as well as inform would-be mentors of the complexity of problems faced by many at-risk youths.

Out of Deprivation and Abuse a Mentor is Born: Monekka the Resilient Teen Mother:

I was born Monekka to Mary and Rob. I am the oldest of four children. My father was never involved in my upbringing. My mother raised all four children by herself. Only two of my siblings have the same father. **My mother did not have a chance to further her education because she was raising us**. We were poor, although my mother worked two jobs, and sometimes three. Because she worked so much, she was forced to leave us in the care of family and friends. During these sittings, I was being sexually molested. It started at age five and lasted until I was eleven. I never told my mother of my molestation until I was twenty years old. I was afraid of my mother. I thought she would become angry or blame me for the abuse.

Because my mother's education was limited, she was unable to help me and my siblings with our homework. As a result, I was a horrible student. My reading and math abilities were almost nonexistent. I remember having to leave my regular class at 9:00 every morning to walk with another group of Black students and a teacher's aide to a portable unit located away from the school. During that time, I was kept occupied by coloring. Whenever my teacher displayed the academic works of all the other students, my works on display were the pictures I colored in the portable.

There were many Black children who had to march to the portable every morning. Because of this, I began thinking that all Caucasian people were smarter than Black people. I believed this foolishness for many years, even throughout my high school years. Somehow, I was fortunate enough to have never repeated a grade, but I was not fortunate enough to have a teacher take notice of my academic weaknesses and take time to educate me.

My mother told my two sisters and me not to bring any babies in the house. She did not focus on higher education. That lesson would be learned later, and on my own time. I graduated from high school barely knowing how to read. I virtually had no math skills.

At 19, my mother and I had a disagreement about my boyfriend. As a result, she put me out of the house. I moved in with my boy friend's family, became pregnant and then moved in with a friend. At one point in time, I had nowhere to go. A few nights I had to wander the streets because I was afraid to fall asleep outside. Eventually, my mother found out I was pregnant and she came looking for me. I then moved back home.

On March 13, 1989, I gave birth to my daughter Avi. I was determined to give her a better life than I had as a child. Her father and I decided to go our own separate ways when I was four months pregnant. I thought he would assist me with the child once she was born. I was wrong. When Avi was two years of age, I petitioned her father for child support. In 1994, we began receiving child support checks. The first check was for $3.08 but the most unforgettable check was for the amount of $2.15.

After working at Shands Hospital for five years, I decided to move to Tallahassee to further my education. In January 1996, I enrolled at Florida Agricultural and Mechanical University (FAMU). During my enrollment, I attended classes full-time while raising my daughter alone. I was receiving food stamps and an Aid to Families with Dependent Children (AFDC) check. Since this was not enough to live on, I began working part-time at a clothing store. I was eventually charged with Public Assistance Fraud, a third degree felony, because I made an annual salary of six thousand and nine hundred dollars ($6,900). The authorities felt that my child and I could adequately survive on an annual salary of six thousand dollars. While awaiting my court date, I began working full-time. I continued to attend college full-time while taking care of my daughter alone. Of course all food stamps and AFDC checks ceased coming. I went to court and was placed on two years probation and ordered to pay restitution.

After receiving my Bachelors degree from FAMU, several employers refused to hire me because of my "criminal background." After much persistence to find employment, my patience paid off. I was offered employment at a mental health facility as a case manager. After some time there, I took a job with another organization.

Currently, my daughter is doing well. She is a great student and a loving daughter. She is currently an 8th grade student in an International Baccalaureate (IB) program at a Middle School.

> Throughout my years in college, I have tried to help other disadvantaged women and children cope with the horrors of poverty. Mentoring under FAMU's Role Model Program, I have tried to help as many children I can, but my work is far from finished. There are still many others to help along the way. **When I have helped enough people, and they in turn have helped enough people, only then we would be able to begin eradicating the horrors of being disadvantaged and at-risk in this affluent society**.

Monekka is now happily married and plans to write a book about her life. Employed full-time, and pursuing a second Masters degree, she still makes time to work with disadvantaged single-parent mothers and their children, assisting them to improve their lives. Her daughter attends junior high and plans to pursue a university education when she graduates.

Monekka's story touched on many salient aspects of the lives of at-risk youths and their single-parent mothers. These will be explored further in the chapters that follow.

The cases of Mary, Cory and Monekka help to illustrate a growing inclination towards mentoring at-risk youths. Given this trend of volunteerism begs the following: (1) Can the proliferation of mentors within communities and schools truly change the lives and circumstances of underprivileged and problem youths, so that they can become successful and productive citizens? And: (2) What are some of the major considerations in mentoring such youths? While these questions cannot be answered satisfactorily, various studies suggest that mentoring does positively influence the lives of youth (Blechman, 1992; Stephens and Arnette 2000; Mech et. al., 1995; Coles, 1993; Walker and Freedman, 1996).

As politicians and education leaders – many of the latter being politicians or quasi-politicians themselves – promote instructional mentoring as a solution to the educational problems of at-risk youths, **(1) they fail to address the inequalities in the educational system, and the deteriorating conditions of schools that African Americans and other minorities attend; and (2) They also fail to focus on poverty and its consequences on the lives and well being of the young.**

In this monograph, the aim is neither to validate or invalidate any particular method or approach, nor enter into a protracted debate on the merits and demerits of mentoring. To do so would detract from the intent to bring to the fore the multifaceted nature of mentoring, and the social cultural subtleties associated with this activity. *The primary objective is to present some of the lessons learned from the shared experiences of students and the author, all of whom served as mentors under the sponsorship of the Florida Agricultural and Mechanical University (FAMU) Juvenile Justice Role Model Development Program (JJRMDP).* The shared experiences produced valuable insights into the mentoring activity. These insights in turn enabled us to constantly refine our approach and methods of mentoring. By bringing to the fore some of the realities of mentoring, the simple, the complex, the mundane as well as the extraordinary, the hope is that this monograph can **serve as a guide** to those who seek to mentor at-risk youths. It is also my wish that the monograph serves **to inform and better prepare mentors** to deal with the realities of assisting the disadvantaged. The examples presented within the pages that follow **focus on both successes and failures** of mentoring. The intent is to flesh out some of the realities of mentoring and not to guise the complexities and difficulties associated with this activity. *Not everyone who is mentored becomes a success story.* And, for some, while positive results may be evidenced within a short period, others may display little change over a prolonged period. **Especially in mentoring economically disadvantaged at-risk youths, there are no quick fixes or magic wand that can be waved to change behaviors, instill knowledge or transform their lived experiences of deprivation. Mentoring is a painstaking endeavor that is sometimes fraught with frustrations, but which can also bring about the greatest pleasure**.

Having mentored for over ten years, in addition to supervising over a thousand student mentors, I can safely say that **there is no single approach to successful mentoring. Each mentee is unique and carry with him/her a wide array of problems that are difficult to package into a simple set of rules or a single framework**.

In the pages that follow, the lessons learned from over seven years of mentoring are presented in short chapters. Each chapter points to a particular lesson in mentoring African American at-risk youths and provide examples of how mentors dealt with them. *In the absence of a singular method or cookbook approach to mentoring,* ***the lessons learnt are meant to alert potential mentors to the multidimensionalities of this rapidly growing form of volunteerism***. These lessons can also serve as points of departure when undertaking the task of preparing youths to become tomorrow's citizens *today*.

It is necessary to emphasize that in the examples presented throughout this monograph, I have changed the names of the mentees and their parents to protect their identities. However, I have retained the first, and sometimes the last names of the mentors as a way of crediting them for their contributions. I chose not to include the first and last names of mentors in order to prevent their mentees from being traced by way of the mentors. In addition, many interesting stories on the difficulties of mentoring and the plight of mentees could not be included in this monograph because of the difficulties in obtaining consent.

THINGS TO REMEMBER

- An individual does not have to have a particular reason for becoming a mentor. People choose to become mentors for variety of reasons, ranging from the benefits they themselves received from mentoring to utilizing their lived experiences of poverty to assist others.
- The mentoring initiative cannot be packaged into a simple set of rules or procedures for application to all mentees. Each mentee carries with him/her a unique array of problems that must be addressed accordingly.
- In the process of mentoring a person never stops learning how to be a mentor.
- Mentoring can make a significant difference in the life of an at-risk child if the mentor is able to tap into the mentee's thoughts, feelings and emotions, and to the extent possible make these his/her own.
- Some mentoring initiatives may not result in successful outcomes.

DISCUSSION QUESTIONS AND EXERCISES

1. Other than those given in the chapter, what do you believe are the reasons why people choose to become mentors?

2. What are *your* reasons for becoming a mentor?

3. According to Mary, her experiences growing up African American became the catalyst for becoming a mentor: What is your opinion regarding Mary's reason?

4. Corey mentions that to be an effective a mentor must be able to tap into the thoughts, feelings and emotions of the mentees to the extent that this is possible. Do you agree or disagree. Explain your answer.

5. Monekka believes that by sharing her experiences truthfully, she would be able to inspire other disadvantaged single-parent mothers: Discuss the pros and cons of her belief.

CHAPTER 2

> The lives of children in poor neighborhoods are studied, and their personalities examined and dissected, often with a good deal of self-confidence, by grown-ups far away who do not know them... The life of a child, after all, is made up not of social "constructs" or developmental "trends" but of much smaller things like stomachaches or hurtful words or red Crayola crayons.
>
> ***Jonathan Kozol.***

Mentoring:

Although an increasing number of Americans are incorporating mentoring as a component of their work or extracurricular activities, the understandings and explanations of this form of volunteerism are often varied and complex as the activity itself. Evolved through the ages as a method of passing on training and knowledge from one generation to the other, mentoring has become synonymous with a number of activities which include: apprenticeship, nurturing, teaching, coaching, counseling, facilitating etc., (Wickman and Sjodin 1997; Mech et. al. 1995; Taylor and Stephenson 1995). **Despite its current day popularity as a humane form of volunteerism, mentoring eludes an acceptable precise definition because of the variety of forms and situations in which it is practiced.** In short, "trying to isolate the exact or universally accepted definitions of mentoring is next to impossible," (Scott and Taylor as quoted in Taylor and Stephenson 1995). If you were to ask people who serve as mentors to define this form of volunteerism, you will likely receive a wide array of responses ranging from explanations of particular activities performed, to descriptions of recipients toward whom services are directed. For example, **mentors in the school system frequently view mentoring as tutoring slow learners Math and Reading. Those in business see it as a way to train young managers. And those in religion see it as being a spiritual guide to seekers of enlightenment**. As Blechman (1992:161), defines it: "Mentoring, …refers to a process whereby an experienced individual transmits knowledge to a protégé."

According to the Education Consumer Guide (October, 1993:1), mentoring is *a sustained relationship between a youth and an adult.* The guide continues to state that: "Through continued involvement, the adult offers support, guidance, and assistance as the younger person goes through a difficult period, faces new challenges, or works to correct earlier problems." This definition closely parallels that of the Office of Juvenile Justice and Delinquency Prevention (OJJDP) which defines mentoring as a: *sustained, close, developmental relationship between an older, more experienced individual and a younger person, with the goal of building character and competence on the part of the protégé,* (1996:56). From both of these definitions, it is clear that **mentoring is not a fleeting fancy that it is a prolonged humane commitment**. This is not to say that mentoring cannot be of short duration. It can, depending on the problems affecting the individual mentee, his or her lived circumstances, and the kind of guidance needed. The case of Tanika and Tamara will help to illustrate what occurred within a short time frame to produce positive results. This particular example helps to demonstrate that in mentoring someone, certain peculiarities can sometimes bring about changes in a mentee's behavior.

A Mentor's Influence: It Took Twelve Weeks

It was the spring of 99 when an assistant principal asked us to mentor a group of high school students who were at-risk of dropping out. Included in this group of teenagers was Tamara, a sixteen-year-old female eleventh grader. From the very first meeting Tamara quickly became engaged in idle chatter with the group of mentors explaining to them that she found school too rigid and boring. Asked what she would do if she leaves school, she did not provide a definitive answer. After a pause she said, "Lots of things." "Can you give me an example of the "lots of things" you could do if you drop out of school?" I asked. To this question I received a blank stare. She appeared very unsure and reacted as if she was never before asked such a question. When pressed for an answer she quietly said, "I am not sure." I then engaged Tamara in a conversation to learn more about her.

Tamara lived with her grandmother who raised her and bestowed on her much affection. Within the last year, having lost interest in school, Tamara's grades gradually declined. In defense, she blamed her teachers for her failure. "They are b.o.o.o.ring," she claimed. After receiving four failing grades during the first six-weeks grading period, Tamara made little effort to improve during the second six-weeks. At that time we were called in to assist. Informed about Tamara's disinterest in school, I selected Tanika as her mentor.

> Although smaller in size and shorter than Tamara, I selected Tanika because of her advanced training, and her years of experience as a mentor, which was longer than that of any of her colleagues.

Reporting on her first week of mentoring Tamara, Tanika wrote in her journal:

> Tamara seems to be a very pleasant person but she does not appear to have any interest in school. All she wanted to talk about was boys… Whenever I tried to get to her to focus on her schoolwork, she would do so for a few minutes and then shift the conversation back to boys… I hope that I can get her to be serious about school.

By the third week of mentoring Tanika seemed to have turned the tables on Tamara. She explained:

> Today when I went to visit Tamara I was very firm with her. I told her if she wanted to talk about boys she could do so with her friends, and not to waste her time and mine… How many of your friends had to drop out of school because they were fooled by boys? How many have babies? How many of the fathers are taking care of their babies? She opened her mouth as if to respond but I followed up quickly with other questions. Supposing you have a baby how would take care of her? Don't you think a baby deserve nice things as well as food and healthcare? How would you be able to provide these things without a job?... And most job calls for at least a high school diploma." Tamara looked at me in shock for a moment, then she said: "For a little woman you do have a lot of questions, ain't ya?" I responded: "For a little woman, I am smart. Not only have I finished high school, I am almost finished with college, and I will find a good job. And, when the time comes for me to have a baby, I will be a responsible mom and take good care of my child."
>
> Tamara then stared at me speechless as if I had punched her on the nose. I then got up from my chair, went over to her and with my hand on her shoulder, whispered: "If little, little me can do it, you sure can. You forgot? Didn't you tell me you are bigger than me?" When I said this she looked at me and laughed. She then hugged me so tightly I felt as if I was going to pass-out.

Tanika explained that after her outburst, Tamara's attitude began to change in the weeks that followed, and that she began to ask about college and what she could do to be admitted. After mentoring Tamara for eleven weeks Tanika wrote:

> During preparation for my graduation I invited Tamara to meet some of my friends from campus. I used the opportunity to let her know that if she finished high school she too could go to college. She seemed exited at the idea, (Mentor: Tanika).

Almost a year after Tanika graduated, I happened to see Tamara at her high school. She ran up to me and joyfully explained that she would be graduating and was thinking of going to college. Inquiring from her what made her change her mind about her education she explained that in talking to Tanika she could not help thinking that if this "little Ms. Tanika can go to college [she too] can," emphasizing the words, "little Ms. Tanika." Four years after this meeting, I was visiting a friend at a medical rehabilitation center. There, a young nurse came up to me and said, "Do you remember me?" "I am sorry," I said, "I just can't recall." "I am Tamara, Tanika's mentee, remember." After inquiring about Tanika, Tamara informed me that she went to college and studied Physical Therapy. She hopes to be a Registered Nurse as her way of helping others.

Evidently, Tanika's small physical stature and self-confidence became the motivating factors for Tamara who decided to make life changes within a few weeks of mentoring. Although not common, achieving such successful outcome within a short period of mentoring is not unusual. *Customarily, the duration of mentoring is dependent on each mentee's unique characteristics, and the complexities of the problems that must be addressed.* **Each mentee carries with him, his own unique set of interrelated behavioral and emotional problems. The characteristics makes it difficult to predict the length of time it would take for mentoring to produce successful outcomes.** Sometimes, after an extended period of success, some unforeseen negative factor may intervene in the mentoring relationship to disrupt the possibility of achieving a positive outcome. This happened in the case of Corey and Javon.

Javon, a fifteen-year-old African American youth was already on probation when Corey became his mentor. In violation of his probation, Javon decided to drop out of school. The decision not to return to school alarmed his mother who then contacted us to ask if we could assist Javon. In order to match Javon with someone who could best address his needs, I selected Corey to be his mentor. Six months of mentoring Javon produced some success. Then, came Javon's second arrest. Corey explains:

Some Ups and Downs of Mentoring:

> As we agreed, Javon and I met at the restaurant where his mother worked. At fifteen, and already about five feet ten inches tall, slim and muscular, Javon looked like he could be a great all-around athlete on his high school squad. In speaking to him for the first time, he hardly said much. Somehow, he gave me the feeling that he was trying to assess me for he kept asking about things his mother may have said to me. After I honestly answered all his questions, we decided to meet again…
>
> Today, Javon and I went to the mall. After some small talk, I started to ask him about his life. He told me that he had not seen his father in years because he was in prison. He said his mother has a new boy friend and that they don't get along. When I asked why, he stopped talking for a moment then said, "I don't want to talk about it." At this point, I could see the anger welling up in him so I dropped the subject. I then shifted the conversation to sports, which seemed to provide Javon some relief. When I dropped him home, I asked his mother if she would allow Javon to accompany me to Williston, my hometown and she agreed…
>
> Javon was so excited to go to Williston, he called me every day of the week to make sure I had not changed my mind about going home for the weekend… On Friday, I picked up Javon on my way to Williston. While traveling, we did a lot of talking so I was able to learn more about him. He told me he has a little sister and that he needs to protect her. "Who do you have to protect your sister from?" I asked him. He said, "My mother's boyfriend. That [so and so] is up to no good. I don't know why my momma still hang wid de fool?" Realizing that Javon was angry, I just listened. In listening to Javon, I learned that his mother became an addict because of her boy friend. "The man", he said, "is nothing but bad for my momma and my sister." I also learned that Javon was arrested because he threatened his mother's boyfriend who "made a pass" at his sister. Because his mother sided with the boyfriend

> when his sister complained, Javon became angry and physically tried to put the boyfriend out of the house…
>
> When we returned from Williston, I took Javon back to school. Since then, he showed some change in attitude… After several months, Javon seemed to be doing quite well. Although he attended school on a regular basis, he still seemed to have problems adjusting from a predominantly black middle school to a predominantly white high school. I have to constantly encourage him to stay in school especially since he was having problems in the areas of science, math and English. I try to tutor him as much as I can and he seemed to be learning…
>
> Today, after mentoring Javon for over six months, I was disappointed to hear that he was arrested again. In talking to him, I found out the he had an argument with his mother because he said, "she would not stop doing illegal things with that fool [her boy-friend]," and that the boy friend acts as if he was his father. Javon explained that the only reason he has not moved out of his mother's home was because he needed to be there to protect his sister…
>
> I saw Javon a few more times after his arrest but then lost touch with him. His mother's phone was disconnected for failing to pay the bills, and whenever I visited his home, he was never there, (Mentor: Corey).

About three years after we lost contact, Javon met one of the JJRMDP's mentors and introduced himself. He explained that he was unable to finish high school and spent time in correctional facilities for various problems, mostly violating his probation. He also expressed regret for not keeping in contact with Corey whom he said would have "made his life different."

The case of Javon shows that while mentoring is likely to have some positive effects on the behavior of a mentee, it is difficult to achieve success when the mentee's lived circumstances exert enormous pressure on the mentoring relationship. This statement is explored further in Chapter seventeen of this book.

In spite of the challenges such as Javon's, individuals should not be deterred from becoming mentoring. **A mentor may be a child's last**

hope, an influential mainstay in the life of an economically disadvantaged youth.

Today, in many communities, residents view mentoring as a very valuable strategy for influencing and enriching children's lives, especially the lives of at-risk disaffected youths. **Mentoring helps in providing guidance, molding character and personality, promoting academic success, deterring delinquency and crime, and positively impacting the lives of youths** (see OJJDP, 1995; 1996; 2000). Given its broad appeal and acceptability, mentoring has become a popular medium for public participation in at-risk youths' educational success and delinquency prevention. As Stephens and Arnette (2000:11) sum it up:

> Mentoring is often touted as one of the most cost-effective solutions to juvenile delinquency and recidivism. Mentoring programs engage community advocates and volunteer mentors who are assigned to work with delinquent or at-risk youth and their families. Mentors can help create links from corrections to schools and the community. In some cases, mentors help monitor youth's compliance with conditions of parole.

As each group, organization, or community seeks to establish its mentoring program, **it will be discovered that mentoring is a demanding activity that requires a wide array of interpersonal skills. There is neither a singular approach nor a standardized set of mentoring practices that can be used to turn around the lives of at-risk youths**. And, while no mentoring program can guarantee instant or complete success, the lessons learned from mentoring could be used to improve the success rates of such volunteer programs.

THINGS TO REMEMBER

- There is no universally accepted definition of mentoring. In most cases, however it is considered a prolonged humane commitment between an older more experienced individual and a younger person in which the older person guides, counsels and assists the youth.
- Mentoring can be of short duration but this is rare. The duration of the mentoring is dependent upon the mentee's unique needs and characteristics, and the array of behavioral and emotional problems that must be addressed.
- Mentoring an at-risk child could be frustrating, and not every child who is mentored is destined for success, but this should not deter anyone from engaging in this form of volunteerism. A mentor may be a child's last hope.
- Successful mentoring does not come in a packaged set of standardized practices. It regularly requires creative strategies to influence and enrich mentees' lives.

DISCUSSION QUESTIONS AND EXERCISES

1. Mentoring means different things to different people. What does mentoring mean to you?

2. Do you think that the lives of at-risk youths can be changed through mentoring?

3. When Tamara wanted to discuss things other than her academic performance, Tanika asked her a series of questions. What would you have done?

4. In the chapter, it is said that mentoring is a prolonged humane commitment: Do you agree or disagree? Explain.

5. Do you think that Javon could have benefited from continued mentoring? Why or why not?

6. As a young African American male, Javon obviously was wrestling with many problems in his life. If you were his mentor, how would you have gone about helping him with his problems?

CHAPTER 3

The Desire to Assist an At-risk Youth Does Not Automatically Transform Someone Into a Successful Mentor.

Civic Mindedness:

Civic mindedness alone is not enough to undertake the responsibilities of mentoring an at-risk youth. Many adults desirous of helping children at-risk may lack commitment or empathy, or may not have the time to deal with the actualities of at-risk existence. Mentoring the at-risk youth requires commitment, a pledge to assist someone unrelated to you, someone who literally is a stranger and who, in all likelihood, needs guidance and support for an extended period (Walker and Freedman 1996). These realities are frequently incongruous with many enthusiastic and well-intentioned civic-minded adults' conceptualizations of mentoring. Some of these adults are likely to discover that the initial desire to mentor at-risk youths wanes as the subtleties and increasing demands of voluntary service manifest themselves. The experience documented by Dedra will help to illustrate these claims.

A Happy Beginning Leads to Frustration:

> Upon her assignment to mentor Troy, Dedra expressed her eagerness to undertake the task of mentoring the at-risk youth. She wrote, "Today was a very exciting day for me. I was assigned to mentor Troy a ten-year-old six grader. He is a well-dressed young man. His pants are up on his waist and he has a clean haircut. He seems respectful and kind. After talking to him for some time, we seemed to have bonded a little. I really like Troy and I think we will make a great team. I hope we will learn a lot from each other."
>
> Gradually, as the mentoring visits increased, Troy's initial reservations with Dedra began to decrease. He began acting out with greater frequency, much to the dismay of Dedra. She noted: "One thing that I noticed about Troy is that he pays too much attention to other people, rather than doing his school work. If anybody says something that he thinks is not right, he corrects them in a wrong tone of voice… One of the things that I now

> begin to observe about Troy is that if he doesn't get his way, he gets a little angry and acts out." As the frequency of Troy's "acting out" increased, it became more troublesome for Dedra. She stated: "When we returned to the classroom, the teacher placed Troy on two minutes time-out. When Troy got up to take his time-out, he pushed the chair down out of anger. While he was on time-out I asked the teacher what he did and she said he called his classmate a bad name on our way to the library.
> When Troy came back from time-out, he had to read a book to me and answer questions from that book on the computer. Since he was already mad, he tried to rush through his reading assignment and made many mistakes. When I corrected him, he got even madder."
>
> As Troy's aggressiveness increased, Dedra became frustrated and despondent. She became unsure of her efforts to provide assistance and felt like quitting. She explained: "Last Thursday at school was not a pleasant visit. Troy was cranky. When I arrived, he was hiding under his desk. When he came out from under his desk, he didn't even speak to me when I asked him how he was doing. The teacher then told us to go to the library and read two different lessons. We went, but Troy lied to me that he wasn't supposed to read the whole lessons. So, I went to the teacher and she told me it was the entire lesson. Troy and I went back to the library but he was very upset. He didn't read as well as he has in the past. Because we spent most of the time reading, he did not have extra time to play so he got angrier. When I left him that day, I told him that was his last chance. I am giving up trying to help him, (Mentor: Dedra)."

Dedra's frustrating mentoring experience is not uncommon. Mentoring is a complex and challenging activity and should be given serious consideration before undertaking such an assignment. For some adults, the desire to assist at-risk youths stems from their views of school children, especially those at the elementary level, as impressionable minds that are malleable to adult influence and supervision. In the school system, however, where a large number of adults carry out their volunteer activities, many unwittingly become mentors to at-risk youths with varying types and degrees of problems. Since the severity of the youths' problems manifest itself over time, some adults who rush into the mentoring activity with eagerness, quickly temper their desires to confront the realities. As Renee explains it:

> When I was first assigned to Bo, he was looking down on the ground. When I went up to him to introduce myself, he did not look up at me but told me his name. He then began tying and untying his shoes… Bo seemed so withdrawn and innocent I look forward with pleasure to being his mentor. The kid really touched me, his face looked so sad. I know I can help him, I can make him learn."
>
> A few visits later Renee wrote: "Bo said things that I never would have expected him to say. … Bo continued to curse uncontrollably even after I begged him to stop…My visit was very overwhelming and unexpected, but I also became aware of preparing myself for future visits to expect the unexpected because I currently have a mind set of what kind of child I am dealing with, (Mentor: Renee).

Although, shocked by Bo's change in behavior, Renee continued to work with him until she graduated. She noted that there were times when she felt that Bo was making significant progress but would suddenly slip backwards. She stated that after visiting Bo's community she felt that it could be the source of most of Bo's frustration and anger

Experience as a Parent May Not be Enough:

For some adults who have raised their own children, or assisted in raising their siblings, the desire to become mentors is regularly fuelled by the belief that their experiences in child rearing adequately prepare them to face the challenges of mentoring. Seldom do these adults consider rejection or hostility toward them as a possibility, especially because of their parenting experiences, and the fact that they voluntarily provide valuable services that would benefit the at-risk youths. Frequently, however, many at-risk youths develop feelings of mistrust, hostility and aggression at an early age. Raised by their single-parent-mothers under conditions of extreme poverty, some of these at risk youths seem to lack compunction and lash out at others, even at those seeking to assist them. Their aggressiveness and callous remarks quickly serve to dampen the desires of some of the most sympathetic adults seeking to help them. Such despondence is captured by Lasandra. She explains:

> As a mother raising three children ranging from ages four through nine, I felt adequately prepared to undertake my mentoring responsibilities... Today, however, when I went to see Kia, she refused to do her assignments. She was also in a "rare form" because she was very disrespectful. She was talking back to me and being very sassy. She spoke of having a tongue ring and an earring in her eyebrow. I asked her where did she get that idea from and she said her friend. She also rudely told me to give her some money because she wanted to buy ice cream. When I didn't give the money to her she became more disrespectful. She said she is not going to do any work until her mother gets out of prison. She then told me not to worry about coming back to see her. "I don't like you and done come back to see me no mor, ever," she said with anger and walked off.
>
> When I left Kia today, I didn't feel like going back to see her. I never felt so unappreciated and I am ready to quit. Some children can be really mean to adults, (Mentor: Lasandra).

Lasandra's willingness and perception of being prepared to undertake the task of mentoring, and the subsequent rejection by her mentee are not rare. Kevin captures his rejection thus:

> I felt that being an African American who grew up in poverty, I could help a poor black child. I helped raised my little brother and have a son of my own so I felt I was prepared to be a mentor. I never thought that I would have any problems understanding my mentee, growing up black and poor myself. I thought I would be accepted. Instead, all I got from Lavar is rejection and nasty remarks. He does not listen and is full of hate. I think he hates everybody except his grand-momma... only when I told him I played football, then he started to listen. Now, all he wants to talk about is football and does not want to do anything else. This is truly frustrating. I could never seem to get him to do his schoolwork. I don't think I am cut out to be a mentor.

In contrast to Lasandra and Kevin, some adults desirous of being mentors make every effort to understand and deal with the problems of their at-risk mentees and succeed in transforming the difficulties into successful outcomes. This is how Lakeisha describes how he did it.

With Patience Comes Success:

> LaVon, my mentee is a twelve year old who needs plenty of help. When I first met him he seemed like a sensitive young man. After we talked for a while I felt we were going to be able to work well together and that I will be able to provide him the help he needs... but, I had no idea how much help and attention he needed until I worked with him last Thursday. I spent the first forty-five minutes of our meeting trying to calm him down and to reassure him that I was there to help him. It was clear he did not trust me.
>
> LaVon seems to have a lot of mistrust. Apparently, he had a mentor who met with him on an irregular basis and when he left, he did not notify LaVon beforehand. As a result, LaVon became upset because of the way his last mentor left him. He felt like no one cared about him and that I too would leave him like his last mentor. I had to constantly reassure him that I was actually there to help him and that I would not leave him without letting him know. I know it is going to be quite challenging, working with LaVon, but I look forward to helping him in any way I possibly can...
>
> Today, I watched LaVon and some other students rehearsing a school play... LaVon seems to have trouble with the way he speaks and also when he is reading. He pauses at the end of each word, and the way he pronounce the words, makes him sound as if he is a robot. His teacher is aware of his problem and when she corrects him he gets frustrated and angry. I tried to tell him that he should read the way he hears the teacher read, but he didn't seem to understand what I was telling him. I know I will have to work on his reading skills...
>
> This week, it seems as if LaVon has become more comfortable working with me than he was the last few times we worked together. However, he still seemed a little unsure about whether I was going to return to work with him, because he asked some of the other mentors if I was going to be there. When I arrived, he was anxious to tell me that his behavior has improved and that he has been good all week. We then worked on his paper for Black History Month. He was writing about Ralph Bunche. Before

> leaving, I took time to explain to him that I would not be seeing him for two weeks because of Spring break and his annual scholastic testing. I did this so as to assure him that I was not going to stop working with him.
>
> This week LaVon and I worked on his reading skills. He had a book that he was supposed to read during the Spring break, but he didn't finish it. If I am not mistaken, I believe the book is a sixth grade reading level text. LaVon had a little trouble pronouncing the words in the book. For the most part, I felt that he did well, considering that the book was at a higher level than what he is currently reading. From time to time, he would become frustrated and clam up on me as if he wants to reject me…
>
> LaVon does need a lot more practice with his reading because there are certain third grade level words that he is not familiar with… I told him that he should take the book home and practice his reading in his spare time. I told him that he has the potential to be an excellent student, if he could just have some patience and concentrate on what he is doing…
>
> After working with LaVon for several weeks, I asked him if he thought he benefited from my mentoring. He answered by saying that he was glad that I worked with him, and that he had a friend who cared about him. That made me feel that I have actually made some kind of difference in his life…Later in the day, I found out from LaVon's teacher that he would be promoted to the sixth grade…
>
> Since I know I would be leaving, and that he would be promoted to the sixth grade, I told LaVon that I would keep in touch with him to check on his progress. I gave him my phone number so that he could keep in touch with me as well. He was happy that I did this and gave me a big hug, (Mentor: Lakeisha).

Apparently, LaVon had developed a high level of mistrust for his previous mentor who left him without any explanation. Given his learning difficulties, he may have also blamed himself for his mentors' departure. Realizing this, Lakeisha said that she had to be patient and guise her frustrations. On many occasions during the mentoring process, she had to stop her tutoring to reassure La Von that she would be there for him.

THINGS TO REMEMBER

- Civic mindedness alone is usually not enough to assume the responsibilities of mentoring since this activity regularly requires empathy and commitment to assist an at risk youth over a prolonged period.
- Although many at-risk youths at the elementary school level are impressionable and malleable to adult influences, they do have varying types of problems that mentors must address with due care.
- While the experiences as a parent help to facilitate the mentoring process, not everyone who raised children of their own means that they would be effective mentors.

DISCUSSION QUESTIONS AND EXERCISES

1. Do you consider mentoring to be a demanding activity? Explain?

2. Many adults enter into mentoring only to become frustrated within a short time. Make a list of the things you would do to safeguard against frustration?

3. Troy's aggressiveness caused his mentor Dedra to become increasingly frustrated; what would you have done if you were in Dedra's position? Explain.

4. Do you think that being a parent adequately prepares some to become a mentor? Why or Why not?

5. What would you do if you were rejected by your mentee? Explain.

6. What would you say accounted for Lakeisha's success in mentoring La Von?

CHAPTER 4

A Mentoring Journal is a Valuable Tool That Must Not Be Overlooked or Underplayed

Mentoring Journal:

Maintaining a journal is crucial when serving as a mentor. A journal enables the mentor to document the mentoring activity, record observations, activities and interactions with the mentee at each meeting. Moreover, a properly kept journal focuses on both the mentee and mentor. In serving as a mentor, you are entering into the world of an at-risk child, taking with you all sorts of feelings, opinions and expectations; these in all likelihood will influence and impact the mentoring relationship, sometimes from the very start. **Mentors should keep in mind that children, in general, are sensitive to the behaviors of adults, and at-risk youths in particular, tend to be even more sensitive given their lived experiences, their social-cultural and economic circumstances.** Mentors, therefore, should not rely on their memory to capture or flesh out the dynamics of such relationships. Many things are quickly forgotten, but when documented, they can readily be revisited to assess strengths and weaknesses in the mentoring activity, and enable informed decisions.

Capturing a Mentor's Feelings of Rejection:

In undertaking the task of mentoring an at-risk youth, mentors should be aware that they might not be accepted immediately by their menteess even though they are providing free services. For many mentors, acceptance by the mentee may take time. Mentors must therefore be patient and not rush to conclusions or pronouncements about their mentees. Instead, **mentors must be alert to their own sensitivities and perceptions of rejection, and make every effort not to let their emotions affect the mentoring relationship**. Here is how Melissa captures an array of her own feelings as a result of her perception of being rejected by her mentee.

> When I signed up to be a mentor, I was full of confidence. I wanted to help a poor child. As a single mother who raised three children on her own, two of whom finished college, I felt sure I would be able to help any child. When we went to the elementary school today, I was really anxious and felt confident that I would make a good mentor...
>
> At the school, I was assigned to mentor Antwon, an eight year old. Antwon is about four feet and weighed about seventy to seventy five pounds. As soon as I was assigned to be Antwon's mentor, I gently took him by the hand and went to the library ready to help him with his schoolwork. First, I tried to help him with his math assignment but he did not pay any attention. Thinking that he may be afraid of math, I tried harder but Antwon still did not show any interest. He just played with his pencil. I then switched to reading but got the same response so I just remained quiet and stared at the poster on the wall thinking I had failed...
>
> Five minutes passed but it seemed like fifteen, and I was still staring at the poster of Martin Luther King Jr. on the wall. Suddenly, Antwon touched me. "Miss," he said, "can I ask you a question?" "Of course you can Antwon," I replied.
> "Do you have a momma?" he asked.
> I was a bit shocked by Antwon's question but replied, "Yes"... Before I left the school, I found out from his teacher that he was being raised by his grandmother...
>
> When Antwon refused to do his math and read to me, I felt frustrated and rejected. I took time off my busy schedule to go and help him and he rejected me. The first thing on my mind was that his mom was not helping him with his schoolwork, which is why he is not doing well. It was while I was preoccupied with my feelings about his mom, that he asked me if I had a momma. At that moment, I felt a sudden rush of sadness but quickly pushed it out of my mind... From Antwon's grandmother I learned several weeks later that Antwon's mom is a substance abuser who neglected him since he was a baby... *Upon reflection, I can feel Antwon's sadness again. This time I let it be, but I am angry at myself for feeling rejected when this little boy has known rejection all his life.* Was I feeling pity for him or myself? I believe it's both. The truth is, I didn't understand (Mentor: Melissa).

In the above, Melissa was able to show that a mentee's preoccupation with his/her own circumstances can frustrate the mentoring process and give the appearance of rejecting the mentor. **In the process of mentoring, mentors must be willing and prepared to probe and penetrate the barriers of their mentees' indifference or rejection. The emotional pains suffered by many at-risk youths are difficult to assess, and must be dealt with piecemeal over time. A mentor should therefore refrain from making quick judgments regarding the mentee's behavior or the mentor-mentee relationship.**

Capturing a Mentor's Feelings of Self Doubt:

While a mentoring journal helps in capturing feelings of rejection, it also enables some mentors to assess and manage their feelings of self-doubt. The willingness to serve as a mentor does not guarantee self-confidence as Howard found out: He wrote:

> As I recall the first day of my assignment, I was thrilled, yet somewhat afraid to meet my mentee because I had no experience with mentoring.
>
> John was my first mentee. At first I did not know how to approach him or what to say to him. The funny thing is I began wondering whether or not he would accept me or if he would respect me. I say, it was awkward for me to feel that way because I was supposed to be the adult and the mentor. So, I should have felt more confident and at ease, and John should have had the butterflies in his stomach.
>
> As we made small talk, I reverted back to the knowledge I had been taught in my juvenile justice classes. I thought about the practice sessions my classmates and I had on mentoring. After I contemplated on my class sessions, suddenly, I had some idea on how to relate to John and not just make small talk with him. **The key was to approach John as a human being and not as a child who was abnormal because of his home environment.**
>
> Our first meeting lasted an hour. Believe it or not, I learned a lot about John during that short time. He was receptive and open toward me and, from that, I could easily tell that he had no problem with me. This put me at ease and I became more relaxed (Mentor: Howard).

Howard noted that the important decision for him was to approach his mentee as a human being and not as someone who was abnormal. **Too often, aspiring mentors enter into the process of mentoring with preconceived notions about their at-risk mentees. Prejudgments are likely to make the mentor somewhat apprehensive, which, if not resolved early, can negatively affect the mentor-mentee relationship.** Individuals aspiring to become mentors should refrain from making value judgments about at-risk youths. This is likely to lessen, if not eradicate, any apprehension one may have regarding mentoring someone who literally is a stranger.

Capturing Subtle Changes in Mentor-Mentee Relationship:

Since most journals are kept ex-post facto, it forces the mentor not only to reflect but also to regularly rethink on the mentoring activity. Through these mental and physical activities, a mentor will likely be able to capture subtle, gradual behavioral and attitudinal changes in the mentee, most of which may otherwise go unnoticed. Over time, in the process of interaction with others, people commonly adjust to the behaviors of others, especially as familiarity increases and interactive distance decreases. The interaction between the mentor and the mentee is similarly influenced and affected. What may be different is that in everyday interaction with friends and others, we rarely keep a journal for the purposes of documenting our interactions, thereby glossing over or paying little attention to subtle changes in behavior or attitudes. In mentoring, a journal helps to capture the subtle changes in the mentor-mentee relationship. Such is the case of Willie and his fifteen-year-old mentee Jake.

> Jake came into my apartment today and the first thing he did was to turn my computer on and began to play blackjack. Since I let him use my computer before, I did not say anything to him. We then went out to "shoot some basket" with some of my friends. After the game we sat around talking and joking with each other. At first, Jake did not say anything but then he gradually joined in the conversation especially when we were discussing the Bulls [Chicago] championship playoff. Several times he interrupted my friends but because they knew he was my mentee they were polite

> to him… I never thought of it before, but now I am beginning to see more changes in Jake's behavior, some of which I don't like. I need to have a conversation with him about it… (Mentor: Willie).

In preparing his journal Willie succeeded in noticing the behavioral changes in his mentee which came about incrementally. This pattern of behavior he informed me, would have gone unnoticed had he not kept a journal. It was while chronicling the mentoring that he began to become aware of the subtle changes in his mentee's behavior. As Willie stated, "It was only after I began to write my journal that things became clear."

Capturing a Mentee's progress:

While permitting reflection on the mentor-mentee activities and relationship, a journal helps to chronicle the mentee's progress or lack thereof. Past entries must regularly be reviewed and carefully scrutinized in order to gain a proper assessment of the mentorship. Rereading past journal entries may seem laborious, especially since the tendency is to think that regular face-to-face interaction provides more insight into the mentee's behavior over time. Why then do mentors need to regularly review and scrutinize past journal entries? It is for the purposes of loosening up the "sociological imagination." As C. Wright Mills (2000: 6-15) explains:

> The sociological imagination enables us to grasp history and biography and the relations between the two in society.
> [It] is the capacity to shift from one perspective to another-from the political to the psychological; from examination of a single family to comparative assessment …
> …the sociological imagination is not merely a fashion. It is a quality of mind that seems most dramatically to promise an understanding of the intimate realities of ourselves in connection with larger social realities.

Through the regular reassessment of journal entries, a mentor would be able to loosen up his/her sociological imagination to connect thoughts and feelings, or combine notes and ideas which will likely trigger alternative approaches, or provide new insights and impetus for the mentoring activity. The following is an example of how one mentor utilized the sociological imagination in understanding and assisting his mentee.

> Last week, as I was casually reading my mentoring notes, I noticed something strange. Dashon had said his dad sent him and his sister Christmas gifts from New York. He had mentioned his dad several times before, telling me that they spoke over the phone, and that his dad was going to send him a plane ticket so he can visit him for the summer. As I reread the sentence about the gift, I remembered Dashon saying how much he enjoyed playing with it, steering it, crashing it etc., but I couldn't recall him mentioning anything about the type of gift so I decided to ask him... Today, I found out that Dashon does not know his dad and that everything he said about his dad was all made up. Since my mother and father divorced when I was very young, I made up a story that I too don't know my dad, and that I used to make up stories about him just like he did about his dad. He then asked: "You did, ... for real?" I answered: "Yes." He laughed as if he felt relieved (Mentor: Christopher).

Here is another example of how the mentoring journal helped in loosening up the sociological imagination, but with a different twist. After mentoring Tyra for a few weeks, Eryn noticed that her journal entries always contained some statement about Tyra's fluctuating emotions. Since she was utilizing her journal to help with her mentoring activities, Eryn decided to have her mentee, Tyra, keep a journal about herself. Eryn wrote:

> Last week, I told Tyra that she should write a journal to help her better deal with her fluctuating emotions as a teenager. I gave her a journal to ensure that she has one in her possession. I was pleased to find out that she actually wrote in it, and completed the activities I assigned her. I had asked her to write the pros and cons before making decisions and getting angry. This, in addition to the "free writing" I encouraged her to do as a way to get her to deal with her fluctuating teenage emotions. Specifically, I wanted her to write things down so that she can become aware of her emotions...
> [A few weeks later Eryn wrote] I still detect a slight anger problem in Tyra. I am not sure if she is aware of it. I encouraged her to continue writing in her journal and to read it to see if she is succeeding in dealing with her emotions...

> [Later Eryn wrote] I incorrectly assumed that [Tyra] would not take me seriously but I was wrong. It seemed as if she really needed to keep a journal all along because I could see the changes in her. I feel as if I am truly helping her, (Mentor: Eryn).

Eryn explained that her journal became an important tool in documenting and analyzing her mentoring activity, thereby enabling her to become a better mentor. She also said that encouraging her mentee to keep track of her own changing emotions, through journal entries, gradually enabled the mentee to become aware of things that "made her upset."

Mentors Self Analysis and Self Reflection:

As previously noted, while a journal serves to document observations and activities of the mentee, it can also serve as a valuable source for capturing a mentor's own thoughts, feelings and emotions. In so doing, it provides the mentor with opportunities for Self-analysis and Self-reflection. Through such retrospective analysis, a mentor may be able to learn about himself or herself. This is possible because **the mentoring journal becomes the looking glass that reflects the mentor's own Self.**

In the process of reflection on the problems of youth today, some mentors will likely draw parallels with their past. And, as their minds journey backwards, some would be able to experience their own emotional healing. Such a healing process is captured well by Kenitra as she tied her experiences as a mentor to her past, which she titled: *Reflections of a Role Model Student.* In this summary essay in her journal, Kenitra described how, through her reflections as a mentor, she was able to reconnect with her past.

Reflections of a JJRMDP Mentor

> I became a part of the Juvenile Justice Role Model Development Program (JJRMDP) because every city has a neighborhood of high school friends like those I left behind. No one seemed to care enough to help them. As I look back, I can say that the JJRMDP provided my mentor friends and me the opportunity to help juveniles with problems. We should be proud to have compassion

on these poor children, because we know first hand the consequences of neglect and bad parenting. **If we didn't help many young people today, who are a simulation of our friends of yesterday, they would most likely have taken a road to destruction.**

Everywhere we go, and in everything we do, we are constantly laying down breadcrumbs of memories to find our way back down memory lane. I will graduate from FAMU in May. Lately, as I prepare to leave the children I have mentored, and move into the next phase of my life, I have been wondering about my old, high school pals. I've been thinking about how many went to college, are still alive, or are married and have families. My mind became inundated with so much curiosity, I find myself dreaming about the times my friends and I shared as teenagers.

I decided thinking and dreaming about them was not bringing me closer to finding them, so I surfed the Internet with hopes of finding a phone number or address of some of my friends. It took hours and a lot of patience, but I finally found the phone number of my best friend, who is Mexican. We were good friends from the 5th through10^{th} grades. The two of us were inseparable.

Although my friend and I stuck together like glue, we found time to share our lives with other African American females at our school. Most of the other girls were fast, frequently pregnant, and boy-crazy. To our astonishment, my best friend and I would watch these little girls make obscene gestures with pickles, talk about passion marks and what they did with their boyfriends over the weekend.

This is not to say that everybody from my hometown who comes from the projects was "ghettoized." I accepted these girls for what they were and they accepted me. As time passed and we entered high school, we began to change. I never understood the problems these girls had with their home life. Our friends were having babies, becoming neighborhood prostitutes, or high school dropouts. All of us were involved in juvenile programs such as McGruff the Crime Dog, and DARE, but none of these seemed to help my troubled friends.

During the 10th grade, my best friend and I began to grow apart. I found a crew of girls who were much older than me. These girls did not seem to mind that I tagged along with them, but they did not care for my friend. My best friend found a crew of girls faster than she was, and I tried to warn her that they would only lead her into trouble. She didn't listen.

As we hung out with new cliques, my friend and I grew further apart. The last time I saw her was at the end of my sophomore year. At that time, she seemed to have disappeared from the face of the earth. The last thing I heard about her was that she had run away from home. I was disappointed in her because, after five years of friendship, she didn't even tell me goodbye. I always wondered if she was still alive and how she was living. I left my hometown to come to Florida shortly after she ran away. It's amazing; I securely locked away my memories of my high school friends until recently.

After I found my Mexican friend on the internet and called her, we talked on the phone for several hours about the past, old friends, and what we had accomplished since we last saw each other. She said she recently visited her family. I was happy to hear that. I was curious about the rest of the old crew so I began to ask questions.

I asked her about Ladybug, and she told me things about her that I never knew. She said as a child Ladybug was molested repeatedly by her father. Now I understand why she was so promiscuous when she was young. My friend went on to tell me that recently Ladybug almost lost her life after taking a drug overdose, and that she was not looking very good. I asked her about Tracy who had her first child when she was in the 9th grade. I learned she is presently a single mother of five children. None of the fathers stayed around and two are in prison. I also asked my best friend if Cherry was still in New Mexico. She told me Cherry had died from AIDS, a couple of years ago. I inquired about others that we used to go to school with. Unfortunately, I heard similar stories throughout our conversation.

The sad part of all of this was that in high school, I did not have the power or insight to realize that we were all part of a sad cycle. That what is happening right now to the children we mentored, has happened before and would continue to keep on happening? I see the traits of Cherry, Tracy and Ladybug in the children who reside in the various communities where we mentor. I cannot help but to think that their fate will be the same as those friends I left behind. I know I cannot rewind time and undo the cycle of problems my

> friends fell into, but now, I do have the power and insight to help prevent it from happening again. I am happy I served as a mentor, and for being a part of the lives of so many poor children (Mentor: Kenitra).

In 1998, after receiving her Bachelors degree in Criminal Justice, Kenitra left with the determination to continue assisting juveniles with problems wherever she takes up residence.

THINGS TO REMEMBER

- Maintaining a journal is critical to the mentoring process.
- A journal should be used to document all aspects of the mentoring activity, fleshing out in some detail the nature, direction and changes in the mentor-mentee relationship
- A mentoring journal serves as an evaluative and reflexive tool for the mentor to assess his/her own thoughts feelings, attitudes and behaviors as well as that of the mentee. Feedback from such assessments can be used to make informed mentoring decisions.
- At-risk youths are sensitive to the behaviors of adults given their lived experiences and their social cultural circumstances. Over time, a properly kept mentoring journal is likely to reveal the subtleties of such sensitive behaviors which will help the mentor to tailor uniquely individualized guidance.

DISCUSSION QUESTIONS AND EXERCISES

1. A mentoring journal is a very valuable tool for both the mentor and mentee; use it to describe your feelings and expectations before your first meeting with your mentee for it will help you to make comparisons afterwards.

2. Before undertaking your mentoring responsibilities, make a list of what you would like to accomplish and specify time frames for accomplishing them. This will serve as a guide, as well as enable you to assess and refine your expectations.

3. List the things you would do if you were to be rejected by your mentee.

4. Howard explained how he dealt with his Self-doubts when he first met his mentee. What would you do if you were overcome by Self-doubt? Explain.

5. A mentoring journal helps in loosening up the sociological imagination. Think of ways you can use your journal to loosen up your sociological imagination and make a list of them. Feel free to modify the list as you go about the process of mentoring.

6. At the end of her mentoring, Kenitra explained that her mentoring journal enabled her to reflect and reconnect with her past. What do you consider to be the salient points in her Self-reflection? Explain.

CHAPTER 5

An Individual's Understanding of Black Families is Extremely Important When Undertaking the Role of a Mentor to an At-risk African American Child

Families:

The successful mentoring of at risk African American youths necessitates an understanding of the families out of which these youths originate. The absence of such an understanding increases the likelihood that the mentoring efforts would be frustrating thereby impeding success and jeopardizing the benefits to be derived from the mentor - mentee relationship. A major reason for the frustration and lack of success is because of the tendency for mentors to use their own family structure and relations, or their sense of family values as the ideals to which everyone must subscribe. **Generally, families constitute different types of uniform social institutional structures with well-defined boundaries and sets of relationships.** Depending on our social cultural values and beliefs, we tend to view the family narrowly, (as nuclear), or somewhat broader (as extended), in terms of its identifiable structures and relations. These models, however, have their limitations and most often do not adequately represent the realities of at-risk families.

The Nuclear Family:

The type of family most often advocated as the ideal to which everyone must aspire is the *nuclear family*. Constituted primarily of husband, wife and children; the husband being the father and wife being the mother of the children respectively, the nuclear family prizes individualism and independence, with great emphasis placed on individual success. With both mother and father in the household, nuclear families are said to provide children with a greater degree of emotional and psychological stability, because they learn from and are influenced by both male and female parents. Commonly referred to as the intact family, the nuclear unit is seen as morally acceptable and economically the most viable social-cultural structure, to which everyone should subscribe and uphold. Hamer (2001:18) noted that the nuclear family structure "has been institutionalized in tradition, policy, and law as the appropriate familial guide for parents, children, and communities. Hence, the rituals, habits, practices, and values that make up this familial structure receive significant state sanctions and economic and ideological support."

In upholding the nuclear family structure as the ideal, intact family proponents heap blame on single-parent females for children's deviance, academic failures, drug addiction, mental health problems, teenage pregnancies and aggressive and criminal behaviors (see Popenoe, 1996; Yoest, 1996; Whitehead, 1997; Mackey, 1997; Maginnis, 1997; Horn 1999). Influenced by Moynihan, who saw delinquency and youth violence as the direct consequences of families in which women dominated, these advocates maintain that the absence of African American fathers from families creates voids in children's lives, leaving them without role models to emulate. As Wade Horn, the President of the National Fatherhood Initiative claims:

> Children living in homes where fathers are absent are far more likely to be expelled from or drop out of school, develop emotional and behavioral problems, commit suicide, and fall victim to child abuse or neglect. The males are far more likely to become violent criminals. As a matter of a fact, men who grew up without dads currently represent 70 percent of the prison population serving long-term sentences (Horn 1999:39).

In contrast to intact family proponents, Nathan McCall in his national bestseller M*akes Me Wanna Holler* (1994:87) states:

> I never heard my friends say they wanted to be like their fathers when they grew up. Why would we want that when we knew our fathers were catching hell? That would be like saying we wanted to catch hell, too. If anything, we wanted to be the o*pposite* of our fathers...
>
> That's why I shake my head when I hear the so-called social experts harping on the problems of black single-parent households. They don't seem to understand that the problems go

> deeper than that. A two-parent home is no better off than a single parent one if the father is… [messed] up in the head and beaten down. There's nothing mare dangerous and destructive in a household than a frustrated, oppressed black man.

If media accounts and tailored visual portrayals are sources for validating our views of delinquency and crime, then it becomes easy to subscribe to intact family advocates claim that children from single parent households are the principal perpetrators of the social ills of youth. And, if we take into consideration that females head a large proportion of African American families, then it would be simple to link the social ills of youth to what many social scientists refer to as the Black matriarchy. While such a deduction may appear logical, it becomes difficult to validate, particularly when we take into consideration that: *(i) many successful African American men and women were raised by their single-parent mothers or grandmothers; and (ii) throughout their history, African Americans struggled against persistent poverty and various forms of oppression to raise and safeguard their children.* To infer, therefore, that the female centered Black family produces a major proportion of problem youths is to deny the historical significance and resilience of African American women, which extend from bondage to present day. Staples (1999:41), captures this distinction well when he said:

> Historically, the Black woman has been a bulwark of strength in the Black community. From the time of slavery onward, she has resisted the destructive forces she has encountered in American society. During the period of slavery she fought and survived the attacks on her dignity by the slave system, relinquished the passive role ascribed to members of her gender to ensure the survival of her people, and tolerated the culturally induced irresponsibility of her man in recognition of this country's relentless attempts to castrate him.

Given their struggles for survival, their history of resiliency, and their enduring loyalty and devotion to their families, why is it that African American female heads of families have become the scapegoats of the social ills of youth? The answer seems to reside in Americans subscription to the nuclear family as the ideal. This family structure of husband, wife and children living in the same household may seem to work well for the middle class but not for lower class African Americans. To put it bluntly, economically disadvantaged African Americans do not subscribe to the narrow view that one's family is consisted primarily of husband, wife and children. Upholding the nuclear family as the ideal is to deny the network of kins that is vital to one's social and economic existence (McAdoo, 1982; Palmer, 1998; Staples, 1999; Hill, 1999; Collins, 1999).

Restrictiveness of the Nuclear Family:

As a mentor of economically disadvantaged African American youths, it is counterproductive to formulate opinions, or conceptualize African American families within the context of the nuclear family framework and ideals. Simply put, it is foolhardy to use a model that does not apply or fit? To utilize the nuclear model as the ideal for disadvantaged African Americans is to be oblivious to the network of kin relationships that are unique and significant to this cultural group (Billingsley, 1968; Jewel, 1998; Collins, 1999; Staples, 1999; Lempert, 1999). African Americans network of kin relationships is rooted in the very history and economic conditions of American society. From the early days of plantation production, the precarious mode of survival forced Blacks to modify or reconstruct their indigenous African culture to cope with the harsh social and economic realities of a commoditized existence (Jewel, 1988; Blackwell, 1991). Out of the struggles for survival, " … an intricate web of kin relationships and a precarious family life evolved over time, reflecting the needs of the black population and drawing its inspiration from African traditions and the realities of life in the quarters and in America as a whole," (Palmer, 1998:93).

Today, the network of kin relationships has given rise to a unique array of family forms based on biological and fictive ties, especially among economically disadvantaged African American families. As Staples (1999:153) explains: "The functions of the kinship groups to Blacks is so important that many non-blood relatives are referred to and regarded as kinsmen. Usually this is a special friendship in which the norms, claims, obligations, and loyalties of the kin relationships are operative, such as those of godmothers or play brothers." Such propensity to establish and uphold familial relations and arrangements seem to fit well with Levin's broader definition of the family as made up of "individuals who by birth, adoption, marriage, or declared commitment share deep personal connections and are mutually entitled to receive and obligated to provide support of various kinds to the extent possible, especially in times of need," (Carol Levine, as quoted in Macklin, 1992:71).

Given African American families tendency to incorporate non-blood members into its extended structure, it is not unusual for mentors to be gradually integrated into the family group. When this occurs, mentors can become overwhelmed by the warmth and respect they receive from family members. Initially, accommodation into the family may create some uneasiness for some mentors, but they quickly adjust when they realize the sincerity with which they are accepted. The following captures Telly's inclusion into his mentee's extended family.

A Mentor Becomes an Extended Family Member:

> When Lewis's grandmother requested mentoring assistance for her grandson, Telly offered to be his mentor. Upon discovering that Lewis was neglected by his mother, and that his elderly maternal grandmother filled the role of his primary caretaker, Telly began to regularly update Lewis' grandmother on his progress. Since Lewis was suffering from behavioral and academic problems, Telly made every effort to become his friend, constantly encouraging him to do well. Within two months of the mentoring relationship, Telly's influence on Lewis' behavior and academic performance was becoming noticeable. Thankful for the positive changes she saw in her grandson, Lewis' grandmother invited Telly to a Sunday dinner, which he reluctantly accepted.
>
> At the dinner, Telly was shocked at the reception he received. As he explained:
> "Lewis' grandmother, his mother and siblings made me feel so comfortable I hardly had time to feel like a stranger. Almost immediately they made me feel like I was one of them. They gave me so much to eat, I became bloated… After dinner, they all chatted with me as if I was Lewis' uncle. When I left, they even packed food for me to take home."

By the end of the semester, Telly was almost fully integrated Lewis' extended family. Telly explained:

> "I went to Lewis' grandmother for Thanksgiving. As soon as I arrived she greeted me with a great big hug. When she introduced me to members of the family I had not met before, they all came forward smiling as if they already knew me. "This is Telly I tole y'all bout," she said. It did not take long for members of the family to talk as if they have known me for years. They told their stories without excluding me. They acted as if I knew what they were referring to. Truly, it was an amazing experience… Before I left that evening, Lewis' grandmother told to me. "Come back soon," and, don't be no strainja," and that I was part of the family. I left that night thinking how much a part of Lewis' family I have become in such a short while. They may be poor, but they are truly beautiful people."

The above example of Telly's acceptance into his mentee's extended family touches on a salient aspect of African American families, that is, the centrality of the grandmother. In the process of mentoring at-risk African American youths, many mentors would find themselves coming in contact with grandmothers. Especially if they live in close proximity, grandmothers are actively involved in the socialization of grandchildren and great-grandchildren. It is therefore important for mentors to acquire an understanding of grandmothers' importance in the family, and particularly their influences in the lives of the young.

The Centrality of Grandmothers in African American Families:

Peering in from the outside, many social scientists tend to characterize the African American family as matriarchal because of the preeminence of the elderly female within the unit (Moynihan, 1965; Popenoe, 1996). By definition, matriarchal signifies the dominance of the eldest female, someone who holds a position of authority and wields influence over family affairs. Besides being stereotypical, such outsider's view also fails to apprehend the centrality of women in African American families, and most importantly, the significance of the elderly female in her role of grandmother, (Collins 1999, Staples 1999).

In African American families, especially those considered economically disadvantaged, grandmothers have become the exemplars of resilience and stability, particularly the maternal grandmothers. Known for their multiple roles as managers, mediators, primary caretakers of grandchildren and nurturers, African American grandmothers are the mainstay of many households. Perry (1999:73-74) explains the relationship this way:

> Exchanges of services are common within the African-American family, and elderly females tend to play a major role. The older adult is often responsible for maintaining the kinship network of the extended family, planning family celebrations, and providing childcare... According to the available literature about the extended family relationships of older Black females, family members tend to interact frequently and have close affective bonds. Pooling limited resources in multigenerational households has been a common practice among Black families. Older African-American women, in general, tend to interact frequently and affectively with family members and are simultaneously involved in the roles of parents, grandparent, and great-grandparent.

African American grandmothers are idolized for their unconditional love, devotion to children, and strength to endure even under severe economic and emotional circumstances (Staples 1999). At several of our small meetings to address the problems of at-risk youths, grandmothers often constituted a third to one half of the twenty to thirty attendees. Many gave emotional testimonies of the difficulties they experienced in raising their grandchildren or great-grandchildren. Despite the hardships of raising the young, these African American grandmothers continue to claim, "They have to raise their own." The centrality of grandmothers in African American families is perhaps best summarized in the words of one mentor who said: "With all the misbehaving and shootings going on, have you ever heard a granmomma get beaten up or shot? Believe me, if this happens then its open warfare."

It is perhaps pertinent to note, that many African American women are becoming grandmothers at an earlier age, sometimes as early as twenty-eight years. These young grandmothers are not adequately prepared for the responsibilities of grand parenting. As See et. al. (1998:291) explain: "The young grandmother is often not financially, emotionally or psychologically prepared to parent a young infant when she considers that she has just reached the point where she is beginning to enjoy life, and establish and work toward her own goals which have been on hold because of her own parenting responsibilities."

As the population of young grandmothers continues to increase, great-grandmothers are stepping in to fill the void of grand parenting, thereby reformulating and reaffirming the centrality of the elderly female within the African American family system. *However, the increase in the number of great-grandmothers reaching out to care for their great-grandchildren is not enough to offset the growth in the number of young grandmothers who refuse to shoulder the responsibilities of raising grandchildren.* Such changing familial trend has increasingly left more and more young mothers to raise their own children in a state of growing poverty.

THINGS TO REMEMBER

- The families of at-risk youths are varied and not likely to fit the ideal family model upheld my mainstream society.
- Mentors must be aware at all times that the majority of at-risk youths do not come from intact families in which both parents are present. These youths therefore seldom share the same values and ideals as children from two parent families.
- Mentoring practices that utilizes the ideals of the nuclear family to assess the needs or deficiencies of the mentee and guide the delivery of mentoring services is likely to result in failure.
- It is necessary to understand the mentee's family structure and relations, and especially the roles' mothers and grandmothers play in the life of at-risk youth.
- Although their statuses and roles in the family have suffered some erosion over the years, grandmothers continue to wield significant influence over the lives of at-risk children and grandchildren. This group of adults, although eroding, holds

much sway in the family and should not be overlooked as important contributors to the mentoring process.

DISCUSSION QUESTIONS AND EXERCISES

1. In your opinion, should the intact nuclear family model be used as the framework for evaluating African American families?

2. African American families regularly incorporate non-blood individuals as members of their extended groups: If you were incorporated as a member of your mentee's extended family group, what would you do? Explain.

3. Knowing the centrality of grandmothers within the African American family system, it would be beneficial to assess the level of influence the grandmother has on your mentee's daily life. Design a simple interview that would enable you to obtain some preliminary information from your mentee, his/her mother and grandmother. This would facilitate the subsequent gathering of additional information if it becomes necessary.

4. According to this chapter African American grandmothers are getting younger: How is this likely to affect the at-risk youth population. Explain.

CHAPTER *6*

The contempt for my people-every assumption, insult, and slur-was trimmed and tailored for my infant shoulders before I was even born. A culture of low expectation, violence disrespect, and degradation, which imposed from the outside, began germinating in the earliest moments of my life. An environment saturated with raw immortality enveloped me as soon as I entered the world ***(Carl Upchurch).***

At risk Youths Do Not Constitute A Homogeneous Cluster of Youngsters With Like Characteristics

At Risk:

The number of disadvantaged African American youths designated to be at-risk increases almost daily. **Despite the at-risk designation, everyday explanations and usages of the term are still hazy. At-risk has no universally accepted meaning or precise definition**. If you were to query people who regularly use the term, you will discover that they attach meanings and interpretations to it in accordance with their professional, social class or philosophical orientations. To truly grasp the difficulty in explaining at-risk, let us examine the varied usages. This will help to shed some light on the elusiveness of the term. According to McWirther et. al., (1998:6):

> **Psychologists, social workers, and counselors** [my emphasis] use the term to denote individuals who suffer emotional and adjustment problems. **Educators** use it sometimes to refer to young people who are at risk of dropping out of the educational system, sometimes to denote youngsters who are not learning the skills necessary to succeed after graduation, and sometimes to indicate children whose educational mastery makes their future school career problematic. **Medical workers** use the term to refer to individuals with health problems. **Economists** and the business community use the term to refer to workers who do not have the requisite literacy and numeracy skills to obtain employment or to succeed in their jobs…
> **We** use *at risk* to denote a set of presumed cause-and effect dynamics that place the child or adolescent in danger of negative *future events.*

The above usages of the term *at-risk* help to highlight its varied meanings. As observed, within the educational arena alone, the term at-risk seems to take on multiple meanings, with primary emphasis placed on the lack of academic success and the non-completion of school. According to Kronick (1999:135): "The term at risk today generally does not refer to deaf and blind children, but rather to those who are not likely to graduate from high school and have a high probability of being incarcerated in jails, prisons, or psychiatric hospitals, or ending up homeless and/or on welfare." **Although not clearly specified, children classified as at-risk of failure or dropping out from school commonly share multiple characteristics which often include low socio-economic backgrounds, single parent families, learning difficulties, emotional and behavioral problems, and diagnoses of Attention Deficit and Hyperactive Disorders (ADHD).** While these characteristics of at-risk appear to be valid, they merely scratch the surface of the complex realities of *at-riskness* for numerous African Americans.

For the majority of at-risk African American youths, poverty is a way of life. As Shirley Hill (1999:90) noted: not only do African American children, "have much higher rates of poverty than white children, they are more likely to live in families that are stigmatized as dysfunctional and in communities with high rates of crime and drug dependency, (Shirley Hill, 1999:90). Originating primarily from single parent households, many at-risk African American youths start their lives with deficiencies ranging from mal-nourishment and drug addiction to low birth-weight and health problems. Detached from their fathers, these youths come under the influences of adult males, primarily their grandfathers and uncles who customarily step in to fill the void of fatherlessness (Lempert, 1999; Hammer, 2001, McWright, 2002). However, in the absence of male kins, some at-risk youths regularly fall under the influences of neighborhood drug dealers and hustlers, thereby intensifying their at-riskness.

Despite some common characteristics, **at-risk youths do not constitute a homogeneous cluster of youngsters with a uniform set of distinctive emotional and behavioral characteristics**. Given the varied characteristics of at-risk youths, and the complexity and unpredictability in emotional and behavioral patterns, it is more fitting to conceptualize at-riskness on a continuum, in terms of the degree of severity (see McWirther et. al). **Such a depiction will help**

to better prepare someone to become a mentor and facilitate a mapping of the mentoring process. It will also aid an assessment of mentees level of at-riskness which should be undertaken early in the mentoring process, and regularly revised for the effective delivery of mentoring services.

Low Risk African American Youths:

Low risk African American youths customarily originate from disadvantaged families that range from late-teenage/young-adult single-parent to two-parent households. Residing in mixed lower middle class – upper low income neighborhoods, these youths are considered to be at low risk of: failure, dropping out of school, becoming a parent, or turning to a life of delinquency and crime. Raised by parent(s) who at a minimum have completed high school, low risk youths are likely to have some academic instruction incorporated in their lives, albeit on an inconsistent basis. Read to in their early years, low risk youths are likely to receive parental encouragement to read on their own, and to value education and economic success.

With their parent(s) employed in low to low-middle income jobs which keep them away from home for a greater part of the day and sometimes on week-ends, low risk youths may be subjected to inadequate and often times inconsistent parental supervision and control. Their anger and aggression are likely to be held in check by various disciplinary methods, which may at times border on abuse. Socialized in this fashion, some experience confusion regarding the relations of power and authority and how these are played out in the larger society. As a result, some low risk youths may be predisposed to reject or disobey formal authority that seeks to exert control over their behaviors. This includes the formal authority of the school system.

High Risk African American Youths:

High-risk youths share some of the characteristics of the low risks, but have additional characteristics that place them at greater risk. Born to out-of-wedlock high school dropout middle-teenage mothers, they may know their fathers or receive some paternal support. Raised primarily by their single-parent mothers and/or grandmothers, they sometimes experience varying degrees of deprivation, including neglect and/or abuse at an early age. As these youths grow older, their lived circumstances create frustration and anger, which increasingly find expression in various forms of aggression and problem behaviors. Most often than not, high-risk youths are likely to receive punishment as a method of control for their anger and aggression. Instead of producing acceptable behavior, punishment creates resentment and furthers aggression. As a result, these youths become embroiled in conflict with their peers and teachers. To a greater extent than the low risk, high risk youths experience higher levels of frustration and disenchantment with academic learning which place them on the brink of dropping out of school, especially as they approach the higher grade levels. And while they, like the low risks are predisposed to reject or disobey formal authority, they are more prone to challenge those who seek to control their behaviors with greater frequency than the low risk youths.

Severely At-Risk Risk African Americans:

The severely at-risks youths can be characterized as those designated as being disadvantaged from the time of birth. On the continuum of at-riskness these would be, low birth weight babies, those born with drug or alcohol addiction or other physiological and neurological deficiencies. Born to poor, young teenage mothers who are themselves in their youth and lack parenting skills, these babies, exposed to inadequate care, grow up with many deficits that place them at-risk of failure in school and in society (see Ferrara 2002). These severely at-risk are perhaps best captured in the words of Franklin when he wrote:

… because many African Americans experience the effects of poverty, ignorance, racism and numerous social dislocations, large numbers of African American infants do not enter the world as socially neutral organisms; instead they enter the world with physiological and neurological deficits, which often translate into social deficits. These social deficits render functioning in mainstream society nearly impossible for many African American youth (1999:248).

Raised primarily by their youthful parents - with some assistance from grandparents - many severely at-risk youths regularly experience physical and emotional abuse, which in some instances is coupled with sexual abuse. For many of the severely at-risk, their best meals are either obtained at school, or at the community network centers in their neighborhoods. Given minimal guidance in their daily lives, they become unable to differentiate acceptable and unacceptable behaviors. Many have never seen their fathers. Unable to cope with their life circumstances, many turn to delinquency and crime at an early age. Within their communities, the local role models are the wheeler-dealers they see dressed in expensive clothing and jewelry, driving around in flashy vehicles in and out of their neighborhoods (see Upchurch 1996; Majors and Billson, 1992). In some instances, they have seen the impact of drugs and violence in their neighborhoods, but do not quite understand. Most have limited future aspirations, and attending college has never crossed their minds or is something remotely possible. By ages seven or eight, some already become entangled in the juvenile justice system.

Trying to capture all the elements and dimensions of at-risk in a few continuous and overlapping categories is almost an impossible task, given the fluidity and complexity of at-riskness. And, even with these characterizations, there are going to be limitations because of the hidden dimensions of at-risk. **In mapping out their mentees level of at-riskness, mentors need to take heed that the categories of at-risk are not exclusive, and that some characteristics of at-riskness are likely to be found in all of the categories but in varying degrees.**

THINGS TO REMEMBER

- Mentors need to be alert to the varied definitions of at-risk.
- At-risk children do not constitute a homogeneous group with a uniform set of distinctive emotional and behavioral characteristics.
- At-risk children can best be assessed on a continuum from low to severely at risk in which the levels of *at-riskness* have some overlapping characteristics.
- Each at-risk youth has his/her own level of *at-riskness* which should be assessed in the early stages of mentoring and reevaluated throughout the process.
- By being alert to the level of *at-riskness* of their mentees, mentors would be able to adequately assess the mentees' problems and focus mentoring assistance.

DISCUSSION QUESTIONS AND EXERCISES

1. On the continuum of risk, three types of at-risks were identified: Do you think there are more. Explain.

2. In deciding to mentor a youth, would his/her level of risk influence your decision? Why or why not. Explain.

3. Supposing you were just assigned your mentee, how would you go about assessing his/her risk level?

4. You are called upon to mentor a severely at-risk youth: What are some of the things would you do to prepare you for the task ahead? Keep in mind that there is no singular correct approach to mentoring.

CHAPTER 7

Mentors Must Keep in Mind That Single Parent Families Are a Complex Group and Not a Monolithic Dysfunctional Unit.

Misrepresentations of Single-Parent Families:

Mentors must not enter the field of mentoring with stereotypic perceptions of disadvantaged African American families already tucked away in their minds. Influenced by mainstream social cultural values and beliefs, media representations, social science or political accounts, the prevailing perception is that disadvantaged families constitute a monolithic mass of single-parent-welfare-mothers who have little or no desires to work their way out of poverty. These misrepresentations and stereotypic views, instilled in us over a prolonged period, have resulted in the formation of negative single-parent mindset. Depicting African American single-parent families negatively is not a recent phenomenon. Historically characterized as matriarchal units that lack strong male influence, many social scientists and social commentators portray African American families the major producers of delinquent youths, (Horn, 1999, McClanahan 1994; Popenoe 1996; Yoest 1996; Maginnis 1997).

Stereotypic Views of Single-Parent Families:

In undertaking a keen examination of African American families, a mentor would discover the stereotypic misrepresentations that have come to pervade our thinking and shape our views and perceptions of these families. Although female heads of household predominate among disadvantaged African Americans, these single-parent families cannot be grouped and described as a monolithic unit with the same set of characteristics. Single parent families may share many common characteristics but they do not constitute a homogeneous group. As Hill (1999:13) noted: "Single-parent black families are often seen as all being alike, typically as families headed by welfare-dependent teenage mother, and marital status erroneously becomes the basis for viewing families as weak or stable, functional or dysfunctional." In many ways, single-parent families differ in terms of their self-definitions and outlook in life which links back to their personal beliefs, goals and aspirations. Overlooking the characteristics that set them apart, many social scientists frequently group single-parent families into a single category, in terms of their deviations from the Euro-centric nuclear family ideals. They then proceed to discuss them in negative terms such as dysfunctional families.

As used in the social science literature, the term dysfunctional refers to family pattern and relationships that deviate from the nuclear family ideals. Deviations such as becoming out-of-wedlock teenage parents are believed to have negative consequences on children thus rendering the family dysfunctional. Given the term's association with the economically disadvantaged, it is not difficult to understand how the dysfunctional label applies to African American families.

Approaching mentoring with success in mind, a mentor needs to be cautious about the stereotypical dysfunctional family label. African Americans did not coin the dysfunctional label to describe their family relations. It was imposed on them by outsiders who used their theoretical models and framework as the bases for comparison. In fact, many African Americans question the characterization of their families as dysfunctional, and the legitimacy of the term as it applies to them. The frequently asked questions are: "Dysfunctional for whom?" "Where does the term come from?" "Do the people who label other families as dysfunctional, were they at one time dysfunctional themselves and therefore understand the true meaning of dysfunctional? If not, how do they know what is dysfunctional?" "Why is the term most often used when referring to African American families?" "Was the term coined by an African American or someone who is not African American?" "If it was coined by a non- African American, why is it frequently used to describe African American families?"

Sometimes, discussions on the term dysfunctional families turn into a series of policy questions, because of the perception that it is tied to "Welfare" recipients. Here are examples of the questions posed by students who served as mentors for more than two years. They asked: "What is more dysfunctional than policy makers' refusal to grant the elderly grandmother medical assistance? What is more dysfunctional when policy makers deny day-care assistance to the struggling single-parent-female and then prosecute her for leaving her children unattended to go to her minimum wage job? Aren't the policy makers who make bad policies themselves dysfunctional? Who is more dysfunctional, the person who labels and punishes the young mother and elderly grandmother, or the young mother and grandmother who are labeled and even stigmatized, for striving to eke out the family's existence in the face of discrimination and ridicule?"

The questions regarding the use of the word dysfunctional to describe African American single-parent families touches superficially on the intense distaste and disapproval of this negative stereotypic labeling. To have a better grasp of the passionate disavowal of the dysfunctional family label, and its application to African Americans, let us look at some of the mentors' responses to the term.

> As far back as I can remember, I was told I was from a dysfunctional family because I don't have a father. As a young child, it never bothered me much because I never really understood the meaning of the term, and how it is used to discriminate against people. My mother raised me and my brother, and taught us to be kind and respectful to everyone. She worked two jobs just to put food on the table, and clothes on our backs. We couldn't afford many things but my brother and I never stole from anybody. From a young age we did odd jobs for pocket money... My mother supported us all the way making sure we were never out of line. Is this what dysfunctional means? (Mentor: Corey, 1996).
>
> Whenever I hear the teacher refer to AJ as coming from a dysfunctional family, I usually get very angry. How does she know? She is not Black. She has never been to AJ's home. I went there several times, and even though AJ's mother was sixteen when he was born, she seems to have taken good care of him and his sisters. Whenever I visit, she always corrects AJ and his sisters when they call me by my name. "You must learn to say Miss Latrice", she tells them. From what I have observed, AJ's mom gives them much love and corrects their behavior when they do wrong. I have never seen her spank her kids. ... I still don't understand why they call families like hers dysfunctional, (Mentor: Latrice, 2003).
>
> I never knew I was from a dysfunctional family until I took sociology in high school. My teacher talked about children from poor, single-parent families and how their fathers are not there to

> support and protect them. Some children get into trouble because they don't have fathers. And, some children get into trouble even though they have fathers, rich and poor. I didn't get into trouble, but my brother did. Because he has a learning disability, he was teased a lot, so he fought back. This got him in trouble. Why is it that families like us are called dysfunctional? My mom didn't go to college but both my brother and I are in college. Does this now make us a functional family? (Mentor: Carl, 1998).
>
> In the neighborhood where I grew up in Miami, we were all poor. Some of my friend and I did get into trouble, and some of them got caught, but we were not all bad because we were raised by our mothers. Sometimes, I can see why some families are called dysfunctional, but I still don't understand. My friend Rob and his brother may be dysfunctional, because they were in some trouble, but I don't understand.... Their sister was the smartest and tops in her class. She even finished college ... If their family is dysfunctional isn't she too dysfunctional? It doesn't make sense (Mentor: Kenneth, 1999).
>
> There is nothing that makes me more angry than when someone refers to single-parents family as dysfunctional. The textbooks say all these negative things about poor single parents. These authors have never been poor. They probably wouldn't know poverty if they see it. When you are constantly told you are from a dysfunctional family, do you know what that does to you? It kills your spirit. It kills what's human in you; that's what it does (Mentor: Moneka, 1997).

The foregoing responses help to illustrate some of the opposition in classifying African American single-parent families as dysfunctional. Given the varying types of single-parent families today, it would be erroneous to view them all stereotypically as a gigantic dysfunctional mass. Like intact nuclear families, many African American single parents have raised successful children (Keith Brown 1998; Hrabowski 1998; Ron Suskind 1998). Similarly, many nuclear families have raised unsuccessful children, some of whom, like children of single parents, are in the criminal justice system. Consequently, to portray African American single parents as a monolithic dysfunctional mass is to misrepresent and underplay the existing realities of this social institutional group. Low income African American single parents therefore, should not be represented as discreet social units, but as a continuum which in this analysis ranges from young teenage parents, to middle teen parents, to late teen/young adult parents.

Young Teenage Parents:

Young teenage parents refer to girls who first gave birth between the ages of thirteen through fifteen. With childcare, food, and shelter provided by parents or grandparents, some continue their education up to the high school level. Others, unable to balance academics and motherhood, drop out of school. Residing with parents or grandparents serves as economic and psychological buffers during the early years of motherhood for young teenagers. These buffers, however, become somewhat attenuated as the young mothers, in receipt of various types of public assistance, subsequently establish residences of their own. Detached from the comforts of parents or grandparents, many become absorbed into what Julius Wilson refers to as the black underclass. Without the necessary preparation to achieve economic self-sufficiency, and lacking in ability to fulfill the everyday needs of their children, many seek comfort in relationships with men who can provide immediate assistance. Usually, such courtship relationships are of short duration, and frequently result in second and sometimes third births. Thus, shouldered with the responsibilities of multiple children, the early teenage parents find themselves pushed further into extreme poverty.

Upon entering the age of young adulthood, and devoid of skills, some seldom enter into the labor market, while others constantly move in and out of it. Some may also turn to illegal acts as a way to cope with their economic woes. Kept on the brink of subsistence existence, they have difficulty in looking past their immediate circumstances to conceptualize a future of success. Many become despondent and turn to alcohol and drugs as forms of escape, while others seek out security in the establishment of male friendship relationships. With multiple children and lacking in parenting skills, many become frustrated, neglectful and physically and emotionally abusive. In addition, lacking proficiency in reading and mathematical computations, because of their own inadequate schooling, they are not able to assist their children academically, and seldom encourage or read to them, much less instilling in them the value of education. Solely dependent on public health as their primary source of care, many of these single parents postpone much-needed healthcare for themselves and their children, leaving themselves vulnerable to prolonged illnesses. This situation is often times compounded by their dependence on public transportation, which may or may not be readily accessible.

Tracey: From Young Teenage Mom to Life on the Move:

> The first time I met Tracey, it was as a result of her son Theo's frequent absences from school. Out of concern for Theo's education, and his probationary status for shoplifting, his teachers, Ms. Jacobs and Ms. Knight decided to visit his home to inquire into the reasons for his absences. Since Theo lived within walking distance from the school, his teachers invited me to accompany them, so that they could introduce me to Theo's mother.
>
> Arriving at Theo's home, Ms. Knight knocked on the door and simultaneously announced: "Ms. Tracey, this is Ms. Knight, Theo's teacher, can you open the door please?" I found out shortly thereafter that if Ms. Knight had not identified herself, Theo's mother would have sent one of her daughters to dismiss the caller instead of opening the door herself. When Tracey opened the door, she smiled at Ms. Knight, and Ms. Jacobs, but quickly stepped back into the apartment when she caught sight of me. Seeing her reaction, Ms. Knight introduced me to Tracey telling her that I teach at the university, and that one of my students was Theo's mentor. Tracey then smiled at me, as if this was her way of acknowledging the introduction.
>
> After our first meeting, I was able to visit Tracey several times to follow up on Theo's progress. During our discussions, I learnt that Tracey first became pregnant when she was fourteen. Finding it difficult to cope with pregnancy and school, she dropped out, hoping to return after the birth of her child. Two months after the birth of her daughter Shantay, with assistance from her mother, and older sister, Tracey did return to school but dropped out shortly thereafter. She continued living with her mother who took over most of the responsibilities for raising Shantay. By age sixteen, Tracey became pregnant a second time and gave birth to another daughter Tosha. A little over a year after Tosha's birth, Tracey and her children left her mother's home to live in a subsidized apartment of her own.

In the early stages of her move, Tracey received regular visits and assistance from her mother, an older brother and sister. Struggling to make ends meet, Tracey became intimate with one of her brother's friends who on occasions provided her some financial assistance, as well as alcohol and sometimes drugs. Out of this relationship, she gave birth to Theo. Theo's father continued to provide some financial assistance, until Theo was five years old. Arrested for drug possession a few months after his son's fifth birthday, Theo's father was never heard from again. According to Tracey, Theo's father acted, "as a good father to all [her] children, cause he loves little Theo who he says favors his granddaddy."

By the time Theo was nine, Tracey and her children moved five times, each time for failure to pay her portion of the subsidized rent. On several occasions, she and her children had to live without electricity and phone, because she failed to pay her bills. During these periods, she turned to her sister and mother for assistance. On more than one occasion, Ms. Knight and Ms. Jacobs pooled their resources to provide Tracey some financial relief. In talking to Tracey, it became apparent that she did not know how to manage her finances. She had great difficulty understanding the concepts of income and expenditures. When Ms. Jacobs tried to help her sort out her monthly budget, she repeated several times, "Ah don know bout dees things."

The last time I saw Tracey, she was being evicted from her apartment for failure to pay rent. All three of her children were also caught up in the juvenile system. She told me then that she would be moving in with her mother. She also expressed fear that her mother's apartment would be too crowded, because her sister and her children were also evicted and living with her mother. "My chilren don want to stay there long," she said after a long pause. Asked what she would do, she said, "find a job." When I asked her what kind of job she wanted, she answered my question by saying that she used to work in a restaurant kitchen "cleaning up and doing some cooking," but that "the pay was not good and the work was hard," so she quit after several months.

As I stood and watched Tracey and her children pack their possessions in a few boxes, I couldn't help wondering how she would cope. The more I thought about her future, my mind would race back to the past. Tracey didn't have lofty dreams for herself and children, all she said she wanted was her "own place." Once when I asked her what she thought her children would become, she

> said: "Ah don know what dey want." As I continued to reflect on the past, it became clear to me that Tracey and I never had a conversation that extended very long. I also recalled that whenever Theo's teachers or I spoke to her, we always had to speak slowly or repeat statements. For example, once I asked her if she "usually encourages Theo to complete his homework," she asked me to repeat what I said, and then responded, "Ah don tell him noten." To her response, Ms. Knight turned to me and said: "She didn't quite understand what you asked. She also can't read."

A month after I last saw Tracey, I was told that she moved from her mother's apartment to live in another city where she has cousins.

Middle Teenage Parents:

Females who gave birth to their first child between the ages of sixteen and eighteen are considered to be middle to late teenage parents. On the continuum of low-income parents, they share some of the same difficulties as young teenage mothers, such as disruption of schooling and dependence on family assistance. Becoming parents in the middle teens produces disruptions in schooling at the tenth, eleventh or twelfth grade levels. Since their pregnancies disrupt schooling in the higher grades, many are able to continue their education until graduation, or completion of the GED. Others, with no assistance from family members, simply drop out. The dropouts, unable to cope with the vicissitudes of parenting and the demands of motherhood, soon find themselves relegated to a life of poverty, similar to that of young teenage parents. Nonetheless, the receipt of the high school diploma or GED, does not guarantee employment, or economic security. As a consequence, many middle teenage parents have become disadvantaged heads of households because they: never sought employment, are employed or underemployed in low paying jobs, or became unemployed. And, while some in this group may seek out security in male companionships, others strive to establish more enduring relationships. More often than not, these relationships result in the births of additional children. Compared to young teenage parents, a greater proportion of middle teenage parents strive harder for a better life for themselves and their children. Realizing the consequences of poverty, and the importance of education, they read to their children, and try to assist them with their schoolwork though not on a regular basis.

Qui: From middle teenage parent to gainful employment:

Qui, a beautiful dark skinned African American woman of twenty-four, is the mother of seven year old mentee Ryan. She is third in a line of six children whose ages range from 19-27. All her siblings have different fathers, except for the first two. Qui grew up in a single parent home with her mother as the primary provider and caregiver. Although coming from a working class background, Qui says they lived comfortably in a close-knit family. Her mother worked hard to provide for the family, and made sure that she and her siblings did not go hungry.

At the age of 15, Qui's childhood was interrupted by her pregnancy. Her mother had moved the family into a new neighborhood. While living in there, Qui began to make new friends, most of whom were left unsupervised by their parents. Soon, she became influenced by her friends, participating in their activities, some of which her mother would not have approved of, had she known. During one of her outings with her friends, Qui was introduced to Jerry, a twenty four year old African American. Shortly thereafter, Jerry began exploiting her naiveté flattering her into having sexual relationships with him. Qui became pregnant, but was unaware of her symptoms. Her mother, she said, never taught them about birth control, or sexually transmitted diseases. Because of this, she was unable to tell why her body was changing.

One day, Qui's mother took her and both of her sisters to Pizza Hut. While there, she began to feel sick. After a few trips to the bathroom, her mother took notice of the changes in her and asked her if she was pregnant. Not knowing for sure what was wrong with her, Qui denied that she was pregnant. Four months later, after a trip to a nearby health clinic, Qui's pregnancy was confirmed.

Shortly after the birth of her son, Qui began to have "grand mal seizures." This she said was due to the epidural shot in her spine during childbirth. After a year and a half, Qui returned to school where she was transferred into a program for teenage mothers. While in the eleventh grade, unable to cope with school and motherhood, Qui dropped out. Upon turning age eighteen, Qui moved out of her mother's home to take up residence on her own, in a subsidized housing complex.

Living in the housing complex Qui at first kept to herself. Then, gradually she started to make friends with several other young mothers of her age. One young mother with whom she became close friends was Teca. Soon she and Teca began to widen the group of friends to others who lived nearby. First, they would have parties at each other's home. Then, they started going out to various nightclubs. According to Qui, since she had never gone to any club while living with her mother, "hanging out" with her friends was fun. Often, she would take cues from them how to act in order to look "cool."

During one of her outings with her friends, Qui was introduced to Rick. As she puts it: "During a one night relation with Rick," she became pregnant for the second time. She kept her pregnancy a secret from Rick, until a year after her son was born. When Rick met his son he was thrilled. Rick promised assistance but provided nothing. Meanwhile, Qui has reestablished relationships with a young man she was dating on and off since the birth of her first son. She says that it is not a serious relationship, but that she is happy with him. She is hopeful that one day she will get married, but not until she has achieved some level of personal success.

To improve her chances for success, Qui enrolled in a GED class taught by mentors. After taking the test, she failed the math portion by just a few points. However, she was able to find employment in a department store, and has been working ever since. Recently, she started attending GED classes in the evenings with the hope of passing the math portion of the test soon. She is also looking into acquiring a home through Habitat for Humanity, which she says, will enable her to provide a better life for her two sons, (Mentor: Clarice).

After getting to know Clarice who is similar in stature and already has a Masters degree, Qui explained that she became inspired. She plans to raise her children the best she can and perhaps attend college as a part-time student.

Late Teenage/Young Adult Parents:

Next on the continuum of single parents are women who gave birth to their first child between the ages of nineteen and twenty-one. Mainly high school graduates, college dropouts, and some college graduates, these mothers hold full, or part-time employment, while some are unemployed as a result of lay-offs. Due to low income, or periods of unemployment, late teen/young adult parents are pushed into a life of economic dependency, sometimes for a prolonged period. As young single parents with children from broken marriages, or out of wedlock relationships, they sometimes find themselves unable to cope with the multifaceted problems of their youthful children. Usually, however, because they are better at parenting than the two aforementioned groups of single parents, their children are likely to range from low to high risk, with only a minority at severe risk. As Harris et al (1999: 490) noted, "… mothers with more formal education in comparison to mothers with less formal education provided more structure, verbal guidance, and elaboration when teaching their preschool children a problem-solving task." Such parenting is often coupled with the inculcation of respect, value for education and economic success.

Jackie: From Late Teenage Mother to Successful Program Director.

> I am the fourth of five children reared by two parents who took great pride in their children. I attended public schools during an era that encompassed both segregation and desegregation. It was a trying period for both my family and I, since our nation was undergoing changes, which were accepted by some and rejected by others. Growing up during this period of change had its ups and downs, especially in the field of education, which my parents taught me to value.
>
> Soon after I finished high school, I became pregnant and gave birth to my first son. Having a child out of wedlock was very difficult. My dreams to pursue college out of state had to be put on hold. This was very discouraging. And, with my son born prematurely, I found myself in doctors' offices and in the hospital more times than I can count. Fortunately for me, my parents were very supportive and encouraged me to persevere. It was a long haul, but I tried to pull my life together enrolling in college, and working full time to support my son. There were days when I became overwhelmed but I managed to maintain my sanity as a result of the network of family support. If there is one thing I can say about African American families, it is that they are very supportive of members, especially during difficult times. My parents were parents to both me and my son, and this provided the buffer I needed to carry on with my life.

As a young mother, however, I needed to be on my own. This was almost a disaster. I moved into a subsidized housing complex, but things became increasingly difficult as I tried to balance part-time employment, college and motherhood. There is a tendency to stereotype young, single-parent mothers who are on some sort of public assistance, but I can safely say, I have not met many of them who wanted to spend the rest of their lives on this form of subsistence existence.

As I struggled with college, motherhood and part-time employment, I met a young graduate student. We fell in love and were married. Soon our lives took a different twist. My husband who knew I had a son was not prepared for instant fatherhood upon our marriage. Shortly thereafter, our marital relationship turned to abuse. In the presence of my parents, I had to pretend that our marriage was sound, but then they saw the signs as the abuse became more severe. During this period, I became pregnant with my second son. I thought that my relationship with my husband would improve, but this didn't happen. A few months after the birth of my second son, my husband and I decided to go our separate ways.

It became difficult raising two boys, going to college, and working. By today's standards of describing families through "negative labels," I guess I would have been branded a dysfunctional family, and my children would have been classified as being at-risk. I was a working poor mother with two young children living on the brink of extreme poverty. With encouragement and family support, I completed college and found better employment. Today, my life has changed considerably but along the way, my sons grew up in different directions not because they didn't have male influences in their lives, or because they lack love or role models. They are individuals with their own personalities, emotions and goals in life. As parents we have to accept our children for their individualities, their perfections as well as their flaws and not to burden them with negative labels.

Tracey, Qui and Jackie are three single parents whose constructions of social realities are different from each other, but who share the common status of being as single parents. Given their differing constructions of social reality, they each used different approaches to cope with the demands of being young parents.

While there appears to be a strong association between levels of at-riskness and types of single-parent families, mentors need to exercise care when assessing family types in relation to a mentee's level of *at-riskness* . Low, high and severely at-risk youths tend to emerge of all types of single-parent families, but at varying rates. Indeed, a large proportion of young teenage mothers tend to raise severely at-risk youths but many have also raised low-risk children. Similarly, many young teenage, and late teenage/young adult single parents have been known to raise severely at-risk youths, especially in situations are substance abusers or suffer from some form of sexually transmitted diseases.

Furthermore, it is not unlikely to find various levels of at-risk youths being raised by the same mother, especially in cases where the mother began having children in the early teenage years or is a substance abuser.

THINGS TO REMEMBER

- Mentors should not approach mentoring with stereotypic perceptions of disadvantaged families already tucked away in their minds.
- Disadvantaged families do not constitute a monolithic group of single-parent-welfare mothers who share similar characteristics. It is therefore erroneous to view all single parents as being the same or labeled as dysfunctional families.
- The varied characteristics of disadvantaged families can best be assessed on a continuum from young-teenage to late-teenage-young-adult parents in which some characteristics overlap.
- Early in the mentoring process, each mentee's level of *at-risknes* and needs should be assessed in relation to the family out of which he/she emerged.
- Mentors need to exercise caution in assessing family types in relation to a mentee's level of *at-riskness.* While low, high and severely at-risk youths tend to be directly associated with each of the three different types of single-parent families, there is no rigidly fixed correspondence between risk levels and family types.

- Many young teenage parents have been successful in raising low risk youths, while many severely at-risk youths were born to, and raised by late teenage/young adult mothers.

DISCUSSION QUESTIONS AND EXERCISES

1. What do you understand by the term dysfunctional family? Do you think that the term should be used to describe African American single parents? Explain.

2. According to the chapter, African American single parents are not a monolithic group: Do you agree or disagree? Explain.

3. On the continuum of African American single parent families, three types were identified, each with unique as well as overlapping characteristics. Do you think each of the family types possess additional characteristics not mentioned in the chapter? What are they?

4. Supposing your mentee's mother fits the classification of a young teenage parent. Would you try to assist both mother and child, or concentrate on providing services to your mentee alone? Explain.

5. It would be helpful in the early part of the mentoring process to develop a short biographical sketch of your mentee's parent. Carefully consider how you would develop such a sketch and how it would be used in tailoring services to your mentee in order to obtain a successful outcome.

6. Compare Tracey, Qui and Jackie's lives as single parents and discuss how their realities may have impacted their at-risk youthful children.

CHAPTER 8

Mentors Should be Alert to the Socialization of African American Children Which is Shaped by an Interplay of Two Distinct Social Cultural Realities

Two Realities:

At a minimum, African American children, if they are to succeed, must be socialized to adapt to two different social-cultural realities, their own and that of the dominant group. Hence, undertaking the task of mentoring African American youths necessitates an understanding of their socialization, for it is through this process that their impressions of themselves, and their social world, are formed and developed. It is through this process also that they first learn of their social-cultural uniqueness, and how it fits within, and must accommodate to, the larger and distinct social- cultural reality. If African American children are to succeed, they must be taught how to accommodate, and how to reconcile their two cultural realities to prevent these from frequently colliding.

For the majority of at-risk African American youths, the process of accommodation and reconciliation becomes difficult especially when their socialization inadequately prepares them to merge what DuBois refers to as their double consciousness, their two ness, "two souls, two thoughts, two unreconciled strivings; two warring ideals in one dark body,.. (Du Bois: 1961: 17). Inadequately socialized to negotiate and reconcile their separate realities, their "two ness," African American youths regularly find themselves at odds with the larger society, which then labels and sanctions them for their nonconformity. As Franklin (1999:255) explains:

> African American female and male youth have come to a crossroads. For decades African American youth faced and overcame barriers of monumental proportions that would have stopped the progress of a less persistent and tenacious people. Yet, each generation met the challenges and survived to see succeeding generations accomplish goals that had only been wistfully thought of by preceding generations. A major reason for the survival was

> the socialization experiences provided African American youth by the African American family and the entire African American community. These experiences, imparted to the youth by wise old African American women and men, taught the youth survival strategies. Such teachings seem conspicuously absent on a large scale in the socialization experiences of African American youth today.

To the extent that Franklin's observation holds true, for the purposes of assessing mentees' needs, mentors must first try to acquire an understanding of the influences and impact various socialization agencies have on shaping mentees' social-cultural realities.

Family Socialization:

According to the social science literature, socialization is the process through which individuals learn the attitudes, skills, roles and behaviors that shape personality, and the customs, norms, values and beliefs that facilitate adaptation and functioning in society. Lasting throughout one's lifetime, socialization starts at birth. During the early socialization period, the parents and other family members have the greatest influence on the child's behavior and personality. Since parents wield the greatest influence in early life, children's behaviors and personalities will therefore be shaped in accordance with the beliefs and expectations of parents. In two-parent families, children have the benefit of learning from, and having their behaviors monitored and shaped by both parents. Children socialized in single-parent families are provided opportunities to learn and have their behaviors shaped by only one parent. Among disadvantaged African American families, this single parent most often is the mother. However, it would be erroneous to assume that all at-risk African American children are socialized by their single-parent mother alone. African Americans' network of extended family relations make it possible for children to be socialized by several adults, with aunts, grandmothers and mothers' female cousins and friends acting as *othermothers*, and, uncles, grandfathers and mothers' male cousins acting as *otherfathers,* (Hill 1999; Lempert 1999; Collins 1999; Staples 1999).

In instances where the single-parent mother is a young teenager, socialization within the family is likely to be deficient, especially with regards to the inculcation of male role expectations and responsibilities in boys, and the male influence on shaping the behavior of girls. To buffer the impact of the absent father, many African Americans grandfathers, and uncles, or male cousins, regularly step in and assume the role of surrogate father. Referred to by Lempert (1990), as *other fathers*, these men engage themselves in the socialization of children as evidenced from the following accounts.

> When I became pregnant with Shawn I was afraid, I didn't know what to do. I was afraid to tell my parents, but then they found out. They were mad at first and maybe disappointed too, but they helped me finish high school. My dad has become attached to Shawn. He takes him almost everywhere on weekends, fishing, the mall, the park … He even picks him up from school. The way Shawn talks to him you would think they are friends… I don't know what I would have done with Shawn, if my daddy was not there for me (Erica: Mentee's Mom).

> When I came back from the military, my little sister already had Jermain. I was disappointed and angry at the same time especially since I used to take her to school… My sister was sixteen and struggling. She was not getting any help from Jermain's father so I had to step in and do what's necessary. I try to teach Jermain as much as I can, and warn him to stay out of trouble. Because he is not doing so well in school, and sometimes I have to work late, are the reasons why I asked you to find a mentor for him (Bruce: uncle of Mentee).

While *other fathers* do play a significant role in the socialization of African American children, it is unclear whether their presence prevents, or absence contributes to mal-adaptation or delinquent behaviors of children. There are, however, many single mothers today who independently, have raised successful children. Staples (1999:69), explains the issue this way: "We are all the products of our socialization. I was fortunate to be enmeshed in a community of women who cared about me and made me care about them. They made me want to achieve success to justify their faith in me. For me there was no need for my male kin's conditional love."

A unique component of family socialization among African Americans is the rearing of children by grandmothers. Because many young African American mothers suffer various forms of hardships, which leave some children neglected, it is not unusual for grandmothers to take custody of their grandchildren and raise them as their own. Given the importance of African American grandmothers in the socialization of many at-risk youths, their role in raising their grandchildren and great-grandchildren should not be underplayed. Hence, the next section is titled 'grandmothers socialization.'

Grandmothers Socialization:

Despite suffering erosion over the decades, the socialization of African American children by extended family members is still a common practice. Especially among the economically disadvantaged families, grandmothers in general, and maternal grandmothers in particular are actively involved in the socialization of grandchildren. Maternal grandmothers' active involvement in the socialization of grandchildren is grounded in the very foundation of African American history in which women, in the absence or displacements of men, shouldered the burdens of the family. Children were raised by, or had intense interaction with their maternal grandmother, a practice that continues on today. Staples (1999:67), notes: "As a rule, children often interact more and closer to the maternal side of the family than the paternal. Daughters remain a concern of their family of origin, and their children are often favored grandchildren." Grandchildren socialized by their grandmothers often benefited greatly from the relationship, which Staples (1999:69) explains this way: "Because I tended to be around women most of the time, it socialized me into norms of compassion, tenderness, sensitivity, and emotional warmth. The lesson of my involvement with female kin was the importance of unconditional love."

Staples' explanations of his socialization by his grandmothers is found to be common among African American mentors and mentees who regularly describe their grandmothers as their friends, their confidants, their advisors/counselors, their true mommas, their spiritual guides, their foundations, etc. Here are a few examples of the comments made over the years about grandmothers.

> I was raised by my grandmother who showed me nothing but love. Whenever I got into trouble, she was there for me. She was never abusive, and she understands me more than anybody, (Mentor: Steve)
>
> I live with my granmomma, an my brother and sister is with my mama. My granmomma give me ever-e-tin. We go all over, the mall, fun station and my other granmomma… I love my granmomma, why, cause, cause why, she loves me…" (Mentee: Nekia age 7).
>
> I went to stay with my grandmomma since I was little. She lived down the street from us and didn't like the way my step-daddy was treating me and my little sister… She give my momma hell and took us away to live with her… She give us everything we want and told me I must go to college to help my sister… my granmomma is my real momma, (Mentee: Brian 14).

The impact of the maternal grandmother's socialization on an at-risk African American youth is perhaps best summarized by the response of one mentee. The mentee who was not performing well academically was informed of a meeting her mentor and I had with her grandmother. During the meeting, the grandmother tearfully explained how she struggled to raise her granddaughter after the mother was imprisoned for a drug offense. When we briefed the mentee of our visit, and informed her of her grandmother's tearful comments, she became almost frantic, holding the sides of her head stating and swaying gently from side to side while:

> Oh my gosh! Oh my gosh! I made my granmomma cry. I made my granmomma cry, I made the only person in the world who loves me cry. How could I do that, how could I do that,… because of some lousy grades. [After a pause as if to recollect herself]. What in the world made me hurt my granmomma… All she ever give me is love. She would give me her last penny if I need it, she would do anything for me, and now I made her cry... My granmomma was always so strong, now I done broke her… (Mentee: Agnes, 15).

In the process of mentoring, mentors should be alert to the importance and influence of grandmothers on the lives of mentees. To capture the importance of the grandmother on her mentee Chancel wrote:

> My mentee Keshan was in the fourth grade. He lives with his three younger siblings and his grandmother in a two bedroom house in an unkempt neighborhood… Today when I walked up the stairs to Keshan's house, the door swung open and Keshan greeted me with a big hug. "Well hello to you too; How are you?" I asked. Keshan squeezed me hard, I was speechless. It was definitely a nice feeling.
> I looked inside the house and noticed that something was different. Keshan's grandmother was not sitting on the sofa. I automatically assumed she was not there since every time I visited, she was sitting in the exact spot. "Hey are you allowed to open the door when your grandmother is not here?" I asked. "Oh, she is here, she is in her room getting ready to take us to church…
> Keshan's grandmother called her grandson to come up to the front. "Wow! You look nice."… Keshan was dressed in a yellow suit with white shirt and a pastel-colored tie… "You look very handsome," I told him. "Thank you. Are you going to church with us on Sunday," he asked. "Boy no, she's not coming. And, go in there and take those clothes off before you mess them up," his grandmother ordered…
> Keshan and his brothers adore their grandmother, who always seems to be there for them, (Mentor: Chancel).

While some grandmothers may be in their seventies and eighties, their age does not diminish their influence and impact on their children and grandchildren's lives. In many instances, this influence and impact increases since many adult grandchildren and great grandchildren often take it upon themselves to protect their elderly "grandmomma" or "bigmomma." The role of bigmomma in the African American families should not be underestimated. She wields enormous influence in the affairs of children and grandchildren. As one mentor summed it up, "When my bigmomma puts her foot down, nobody dare says anything. Even granddaddy knows to keep his mouth shut."

Peer Socialization:

Inasmuch as other fathers and other mothers may be able to buffer or mitigate some of the negative influences on children, they may not always be successful in their efforts, (Lempert 1990; Collins). Under such circumstances, many African American youths are left vulnerable to the influences of peers. Particularly for low-income youths, peer alliances are formed at an early age. Girls usually form relations with few friends while boys develop more extensive relationships with a larger number of peers. And, while peer relations among girls focus more on shared activities, those for boys show greater dependence on the group for support and approval, (Harris 1999:81).

> For an adolescent female, her peers provide affection and support parents, especially her mother, is not giving at this crucial time... The more negative the daughter-mother relationship, the more she is encouraged to experiment with male/female relationships, not usually out of love but for fun and excitement, and not usually out of independent goals but in order to conform with peers and their street norms...
> Her sexual experimentation is extensive ... The time between beginning her first dating activities and her first sexual intercourse, and her first pregnancy is relatively short... She is neither in pursuit of love, nor marriage...(Scott 1999:175-176).

For males, peer norms and dependence on peers exert an enormous amount of control over their behaviors, especially as the need for approval and support increases. The dynamics of peer influences are such that as the dependence on the peer group increases the dependence on family members' decreases. Harris (1999:81) explains the impact of peer influence this way:

> The early separation of low-income male youth from parents increases their reliance upon peers for support and self-esteem... Peer norms exert a significant degree of control over members' behaviors and, depending on feelings of loyalty to group norms, can either decrease or increase feelings of self- esteem... This need for approval and support increases the importance of the punishments and rewards, delivered by peer members and minimizes the influence of family values and standards.

One of the most troubling aspects of peer socialization is the tendency for peers to downplay the value of education. Despite increasing educational opportunities, African American male youths from low-income backgrounds tend to equate educational advancement with a loss of manliness, and as an indicator of femininity. As Harris (1999:82) again explains:

> …African Americans who achieve academic success and rarely encounter conflict with authority figures are often perceived as sissified and lacking in manliness. The tendency to prefer academics to activities of the peer group equate to an absence of manhood; the lack of manhood is most always perceived as feminine. The male peer group then, operates under the assumption that a display of feminine aspects of the self is evidence of weakness…
>
> As a result, many African American male youth forego excellence in education to avoid ridicule and rejection, which stems from homophobia and that of their same-sex peers.

While no singular explanation exists as to why disadvantaged African American youths tend to feminize and undervalue education, a cursory examination of the social science literature provides various clues. Among them are: a history of discrimination against African American advancement, the denial of equal educational opportunities for African Americans, deficient curriculum and mis-education, discrimination and racism, poor public schools, lack of employment opportunities.

School Socialization:

As an agent of socialization, schools help in preparing children for future roles, training and guiding them to become productive citizens. While responsible for teaching basic skills and technical knowledge, schools should also play a key role in promoting social relationships and transmitting culture. As Comer (2003:148) explains: "A good education should help students to solve problems encountered at work and in personal relationships, to take on the responsibility for caring for themselves and their families, to get along well in a variety of settings, and to be motivated, contributing members of a democratic society. Such learning requires conditions that promote positive child-and-youth development." To effectively fulfill these expectations, school administrators and teachers must be prepared and willing to respond to the needs of all students.

Not every student who enters school for the first time does so with the same level of preschool academic preparation. Take the disadvantaged African American children for example, most of them begin school inadequately prepared, or with certain learning deficits. Because their economic circumstances or home environment neither cater to, nor facilitate formal learning, many African American children quickly become displaced in the academic setting. Labeled or simply neglected by the very institutions established to educate them, many find themselves left further and further behind academically. Their labels such as slow learners, or attention deficit hyperactivity disorders (ADHD), become self-fulfilling prophecies as they begin to internalize negative images of themselves. As Kendall (1998:142) noted, "In addition to teaching specific knowledge and skills, schools have a profound effect on children's self-images, beliefs and values." Negative labels not only serve to diminish or destroy a child's self-image but also lead them to either withdraw, or aggressively act out in defiance. In the case of La Mar cited below, we observe the symptoms of withdrawal in an ADHD labeled youth as captured by his mentor.

La Mar: Feeling Discredited by the ADHD Label:

> On my first visit to the school, I was assigned to mentor La Mar, a nine year old African American. I was told that La Mar was diagnosed with Attention Deficit Hyperactivity Disorder (ADHD), is regularly inattentive, and very aggressive. After our introduction, I tried to get La Mar to read, but he refused. He also refused to work on his math problems and kept his head down without talking to, or looking up at me. "If you don't want to do your school work, then, let's talk about you, tell me about yourself," I said. La Mar just shifted in his chair without responding. "Since you don't want to talk about yourself, let's talk about me instead," I continued with some reluctance in my voice.
>
> As I began to tell La Mar about myself he would glance at me sideways and when I told him I had a little brother just like him (something I made up) he looked straight at me for the first time. After talking about myself, I asked him again to tell me about himself. I found out that he and his baby brother live with their

mom in a housing project on the South side of town. La Mar and his mom have a close relationship, and she assists him with his schoolwork. Although his dad does not live at home he is somewhat active in La Mar's life. After talking for over an hour, I left and promised La Mar to see him in two days…

When I arrived at his school, La Mar was waiting for me. Again, I tried to work with him on his math and reading assignments but he did very little. After talking about his little brother for a few minutes, I asked, "Why don't you want to do your assignments La Mar?" He put his head down, but did not answer. After I gradually persuaded him to give me a reason he said, "Cause I have disability and I'm slow."
"Who told you that?" I asked.
"Miss Beck," (pseudonym for his teacher) he said almost inaudibly. Immediately, I responded, "No La Mar, you are not slow. Everybody, including your teacher and me, has some kind of disability, but we can still learn. You too can learn. And, you know what? I think you are very smart." Knowing that he loves the Rap artiste "Lil Romeo," I asked him if he thinks Ms. Beck, his Caucasian teacher, knows who is Lil Romeo. He looked at me and then burst out laughing and saying, "Ms. Beck noo, noo, noo; Ms. Beck dooon know Lil Romeo," he responded.
"You see Ms. Beck don't know Lil Romeo and she is still smart, don't you think so?" He shook his head up and down indicating "yes". "If Ms. Beck is smart and she does not know Lil Romeo. *You know* Lil Romeo, so don't you think that you are smart also?" When I said this, he looked up at me quizzically so I repeated the statement slowly. I did not wait for him to answer and said, "You think about it."

As the semester progressed a bond developed between La Mar and I. I knew that I was having a positive influence on him. Now, when I go to visit him, he wants to immediately complete his class work so we could go outside and play basketball together. To encourage him to continue his good behavior in and out of the classroom, I promised La Mar that with his mother's permission, I would take him to one of FAMU's football games. Immediately he began to brag to the other students that he was going to a football game *because he was a smart student.*

On the Saturday afternoon of the game, I arrived at La Mar's home to find a happy anxious nine-year-old ready to go to the game. Although his mother had gone to work, she left a message that she

> really appreciated all the support I am giving her son. When we arrived at the game, we went to the concession stand to get hot dogs and soda. We then sat near the famous FAMU 100 marching band. Both La Mar and I watched the game with great excitement. After the game, we went down onto the football field so La Mar could take pictures with the players.
>
> On our way home after the game, La Mar told me several times that before he met me he felt like he was a dummy, and that he would never be anything because of his disability. I then reached over and touched him and said, "If you are a dummy, then I am a bigger dummy." He laughed so much at my response that he even made me start laughing. When I dropped him home that evening, I reassured him that he is a smart boy and made him promise me that would never again say that he is a slow learner or a dummy, (Mentor: Clarice).

By using herself and La Mar's teacher as examples, Clarice was able to tap into La Mar's negative perception of himself and reassure him that he is smart, and that the negative label placed on him is not an indication of his learning abilities.

Schools and Cultural Socialization:

Apart from being labeled, many disadvantaged African American students must deal with the perception of their cultural inferiority. This perception of African American cultural inferiority even resides within the school system. Schools present themselves as culturally neutral institutions and many teachers claim to be knowledgeable about and sensitive to the multicultural backgrounds of their students. These portrayals of our schools however, do not accurately reflect the true conditions within the schools as these pertain to African Americans. As Brenda and Franklin Campbell-Jones (2003:142), explain:

> In school, more than any other place in society, African American children are socialized to believe that their cultural currency is low relative to their Euro-American counterparts. It is in school that they begin to accept this devaluation as the way things are and begin to "disidentify" with school. Disidentification comes in the form of nonparticipation in school activities, academics and eventually dropping out of school…

> In any public school in America today, one can find teachers, counselors, psychologists, administrators... using these terms [culturally deprived, culturally disadvantaged etc.] as they attempt to ensure student academic performance.

Even though many schools espouse multicultural education, teachers seldom incorporate culturally sensitive techniques in their teaching practices. Instead of tailoring instruction to be culturally relevant, teachers are more likely to subscribe to the practice of lowering academic expectations, or de-emphasizing advanced academic curriculum for disadvantaged African American children. In noticing the contradiction between classroom instruction, and the culturally visible portraits on the walls of his mentee's school, one mentor wrote:

> The first day I went to the elementary school, I was happy to see posters of prominent black men and women on the walls in the corridors and in the library. Knowing that the students were predominantly African Americans, I was happy to see the portraits of Booker T. Washington, George Washington Carver, Martin Luther King, Malcolm X, Thurgood Marshall, Barbara Jordan, Harriet Tubman etc. When I saw these portraits, I felt that the school was serious about educating African American students, but when I went to the classrooms, it was a different situation altogether. The majority of the teachers were Caucasian females... This is my eight weeks of mentoring and I am yet to see or hear the teachers make references to some of the same people posted on the school walls... Once, when my mentee was asked to read aloud in class, he was quickly laughed at by the other students, because he could not pronounce many of the words. The next time I visited, I took him to the library and since his name is Malcolm, I showed him the picture of Malcolm X, and asked him if he knew anything about Malcolm. When he said "no," I then told him the story of Malcolm X, emphasizing that like him, Malcolm X didn't know how to read very well, and how he learned to read using a dictionary while he was in prison. I told Malcolm that he too can be like Malcolm X if he tries harder... Now, every time I visit, he wants to read to me. He is becoming a real show-off, (Mentor: Stewart).

By making the academic material culturally relevant, Stewart not only succeeded in getting his mentee to learn, but also assisted him with his self confidence while demonstrating to him that learning could be fun.

Racial Socialization:

Stewart's observation is linked to one of the most troubling aspects of socialization for most African American parents, teaching their children about the realities of their race. "Racial socialization is the process by which the parents shape their children's attitudes about race and show the children how they fit into the context of race in their society," (Murray and Mandara 2002 as explained in McAdoo 2002:50). While many African American parents teach the children about the realities of their race in a white dominated society, using their experiences as examples (Hill, 1999), economically disadvantaged parents are less likely to teach their children about their race. Children of this latter group most often learn about their race and its consequences by overhearing their parents and other adults in their communities talking about it, or by someone referring to them as "Blacks" or by other more derogatory terms. Sometimes, African American children learn of the negative consequences of race within the school setting where they experience differential treatment from white students. As one mentor explains:

> I was curious as to when children begin to come into contact with racism and their understanding of it.
> The other day, while mentoring, a little Black girl named Taria made a comment that took my breath away. In observing the teacher, Taria said, "She never calls on any of the Black people."
> "What makes you think that?" I asked.
> "She is White," Taria answered. "Her favorite kids are White."
> I was taken aback a little that day by Taria's claims. I was a little sad. A nine year old, pondering over the race issue, paints a bleak picture of the integrity of our society today. Furthermore, it says a lot about our lack of innocence as African American children. With no solution to racism, African American kids must be taught how to overcome, or fall to the influence of racism (Mentor: Daren).

While youthful mentees such as Taria expresses some level of awareness of race and its consequences, others seem less conscious of racial distinctions. Many young mentees may use racial slurs, or make derogatory racial remarks but they seldom understand the distinctiveness of racial groups until later in their lives. In many ways, these youths may naïvely display their racial confusion as mentor Judy experienced:

> A racial difference came out during my mentoring last Tuesday. After the incident occurred, I began reflecting on the fact that I am the only Caucasian at the center where everybody is African-American. I felt that from the children's vantage point, me, being at the center, might be a "different" or "unique" experience for the children. Even the children I spoke with, all have African-American teachers. However, my story of racial differences began while I was playing a word game on the chalkboard with a second grader named Tann. I was sitting in a chair playing the game when a young girl named Lyah began playing with my hair. Lyah's playing with my hair did not bother me so I continued to play the word game with Tann. After Lyah was finished playing with my hair, she asked me if I had a "weave" in my hair. I told her that I did not have a "weave" in my hair, and that it is my real hair. Lyah insisted that I did have a "weave," so I just dropped the subject.
>
> This experience caught me off guard since I am not a Barber. My knowledge of what "weaves' are, and why people wear them is minimal. In a way, I am just as naïve about a "weave" as Lyah is, in her asking if I wore one. A "weave," to me, is part of the African-American culture, but I could be wrong.
>
> I found a lot of humor in this incident, and I think when Lyah grows older, if she remembers the incident, she will find humor in her comment too, (Mentor: Judy).

Although Daren and Judy's experiences regarding mentees' awareness of race differs, mentors need to be conscious of mentees' sensitivities toward racial distinctions and racism. **It is best not to equate youthfulness with innocence about race and racism. A mentor's best approach to mentoring therefore would be to remain culturally and ethically neutral.**

THINGS TO REMEMBER

- Mentors should not dismiss or overlook the fact that the African American child is caught between two cultural realities, his/her own and that of the dominant White society.
- The two cultural realties produces internal conflict for the African American child who must find ways to reconcile the differences if he/she is to succeed.
- At-risks youths, raised in poverty primarily by single-parent mothers are often not adequately socialized to reconcile the social-cultural contradictions in their lives thereby increasing their levels of *at-riskness*.
- African American grandmothers have always played a vital role in the socialization of grandchildren. And, among at-risk youths grandmothers are likely to be the primary guardians. The impact and influence of the grandmother on the life of the at-risk youth should be an integral part of the mentoring process.
- To a large degree, at-risk African American males tend to feminize or undervalue commitment to educational success/advancement which can frustrate and impede the mentoring process.
- At-risk youths regularly enter school with learning deficits and a trifle of preschool preparation. Because of this, many usually find schooling frustrating and painful.
- Instead of overlooking a child's learning deficits, a mentors should seek out ways to address them.

DISCUSSION QUESTIONS AND EXERCISES

1. African American children must be socialized to adapt to two different social cultural realities: Why is this necessary? Discuss.

2. *Other fathers, other mothers*, grandmothers and peers are all influential in the socialization process, outline the socialization process of your mentee to determine which of these individuals or groups have the greatest influence on him or her.

3. Many at-risk African American children enter school with little academic preparation: What would you do if you found that your mentee's academic performance is due to his/her inadequate pre-school preparation?

4. Peers regularly exert enormous influence on at-risk youths: How would you assess the level of peer influence on your mentee? Assuming that the influence is oriented toward deviant behavior: What steps would you take to steer your mentee toward acceptable behavior? Explain.

5. Labeled as having Attention Deficit and Hyperactivity Disorder (ADHD), many children feel discredited: How would you go about assisting your mentee if he/she feels discredited by the ADHD label. Explain.

6. What is your assessment of how Clarice assisted La Mar in dealing with his ADHD label?

7. In your opinion, do you think at-risk African American youths could benefit more from culturally relevant educational instruction? Explain.

8. How would you explain racial differences and racism to your mentee?

CHAPTER 9

Mentoring is More Than Teaching Reading and Math:

Mentoring and Tutoring:

In volunteering to be a mentor, many adults today regularly find themselves being cast in the role of math and reading tutors to at-risk youths. Impetus for such tutorship placements is based on policies that focus on standardized test scores as a measure of educational success. Since such test scores regularly show that at-risk African American youths perform poorly in math and English, politicians and educators alike have promoted tutoring under the label of mentoring as a way to assist at-risk children. The prevailing belief is that these youths would benefit from the additional instruction and attention they receive. Particularly for African American youths, the group most often identified as being at at-risk educationally, instructional mentorship is believed to hold enormous academic benefits. However, mentoring and tutoring are not the same. **Mentoring** takes a more holistic view of building character, fostering coping strategies, and providing meaningful guidance toward success. **Tutoring** focuses primarily on the academic progress of youths. **A tutored child is likely to improve academically, but if his/her personal and social problems, his/her social cultural realities, are ignored or inadequately addressed, then academic progress becomes hollow triumph.**

Discrimination in Education:

In order for instructional mentorship to achieve any high degree of success, mentors will have to be alert to the complexity of problems that affect learning, and how to address or reduce them. Most importantly, they must show a genuine interest in the youths as social beings, and not to view them as stigmatized instructional objects. Having such ethical interest usually requires going beyond academic instruction, going beyond the teaching of reading and math. Several factors make this essential.

Disadvantaged African American at-risk youths regularly find themselves in an educational double bind. Most often, they attend poorly funded, instructionally ill-equipped schools that lack an adequate number of African American teachers and administrators to serve as mentors and role models. Frequently negatively labeled, discouraged subtly and not so subtly, dismissed or simply neglected, many at-risk African American youths frequently become alienated from the academic process. Neither their teachers, nor their textbooks incorporate their social cultural histories into their learning process to encourage them toward academic achievement. Rivers and Rivers, (2001:177), write:

> …African American children often cannot understand how what they are learning applies to real-life situations. For them, life is generally quite different from what they are taught is normal. The information they are forced to learn is not relevant to what they experience at home or in their neighborhood. History classes enforce the idea that African Americans have contributed little or nothing. Instruction in textbook English only alienates children from their surroundings at home. Math classes teach formulas but no reality-based concepts.

Other writers have captured vividly how African Americans were, and still are being dissuaded, or simply discriminated against by the educational system. Gordon Parks in his semi-autobiographical account *The Learning Tree* captures one of the many forms of discouragement in the following passage:

As the days went by, the relationship between Newt and Miss McClintock became considerably worse. He got his homework done and it was acceptable, but she never asked questions of him. And though he thought he deserved a B on the midterm test in October, he received a C. He went to see her about this one evening, asking her bluntly why he didn't get a higher mark.

"Are you telling me how to grade young man?"

"No-ma'am, I am not. I just think I should have got a higher mark."

"Well, there seems to be some difference between what you thought and what you got, doesn't there?...

"You know one thing. You don't like me or any of the rest of the colored kids. I found out you told my sister and brother the same thing you told me-that we'd wind up porters and maids, and you been tellin' all the other colored kids the same thing for years and years. That's why they always make you their guidance teacher…" (Parks 1963:143).

More recently, in 1998, Ron Suskind in his national bestseller *A Hope in the UNSEEN*, captures vividly how Cedric Jennings, an African American student from a crime-infested school in Washington D.C., was rejected admission to MIT. The professor who rejected Cedric then tried to discourage him from applying to Ivy League colleges by recommending him to lesser-ranked institutions. Suskind (1998: 97-98), wrote:

> He opens a manila file and, after a moment, asks if Cedric is "thinking about applying and coming to MIT."
>
> "Oh, yeah," Cedric says, squeezing out a tight laugh. "I've been wanting to come for years. Like my whole life."
>
> There's an interminable silence, five seconds maybe, as Trilling looks down at the file again and then lifts his gaze to meet Cedric's eyes.
>
> "Well, I don't think you're MIT material," the professor says flatly. "Your academic record isn't strong enough."…
>
> Trilling looks back down at the file to retrieve a key number. "I see your SSATs are only a 910," he says, "and right there, that's at least 200 points below what they need to be accepted at MIT."…
>
> Here, let me give you the name of a professor I know at Howard University in Washington," he says, looking down and scribbling, "and another one I know at the university of Maryland. You should call them…"
>
> When he gets to his dorm room… closing his eyes and beginning a fist replay of the scene: of him in the office, of Trilling's words- "not MIT material." Remembering how small he felt sitting there,…
>
> With his eyes closed, Cedric yells, "RACIST!"

Today, many African American youths like Newt and Cedric are being discouraged, not from seeking admissions to colleges, but from enrolling in advanced placement courses, or working hard to get to the next grade levels, or dropping out of school. Reasons for discouragement ranges from: racism to labeling and stereotyping; learning and behavioral difficulties to teacher "burn-out"; lack of individualized academic attention to instructional deficiencies; curriculum rigidity to cultural relevance, subtle to outright discouragement.

Building Self Esteem:

Negative comments such as those made to Newt and Cedric, and other forms of discouragement, serve to diminish or destroy the at-risk African American youths' confidence and self-esteem (sense of self worth). Teachers and school administrators not only occupy positions of authority; they are the first, outside of the home and family, to wield enormous influence and power over these children's lives. Their remarks and behaviors, positive and negative, do impact and influence these youths confidence and self esteem.

Born and raised under conditions of poverty, disadvantaged African American youths regularly suffer from low self-esteem as a result of their race and the stigma associated with poverty, (Shirley Hill 1999). Their mental constructs of negative feelings toward themselves are deeply affected by their lived circumstances. Depending on their self perceptions, some mentees may enter into sexual relationships as a way of improving their self worth. If not addressed, such relationships, instead of improving self esteem, could serve to the detriment of the mentee. Confronted with such a situation mentor Nikeya decided to address the issue head on. Nikeya wrote:

> Agnes told me that she was depressed because she didn't have a boyfriend, and that she was tired of sleeping with different boys. She feels that having a boy friend would improve her self esteem. I told her that we would have to have a heart to heart regarding her low self esteem…
>
> I have much concern about Agnes keeping her friend's baby. Caring for a baby at the tender age of sixteen, she is already trying to map out her life and planning kids… She is concerned about starting a family…
>
> Today, I gave Agnes a long talk about the need to finish high school without having any children; then go on to college or seek out a trade, work for a while before starting a family, - and it must be only after marriage… I hope I wasn't sounding too much like a mother… [A few weeks later] Agnes informed me that it has been a long time since she had a sexual relationship with anyone. I complemented her…

Some times, the problem of mentees' low self esteem is exacerbated by the insensitivities and negative remarks of their teachers and school administrators. Among the negative remarks made by teachers and/or administrators, and overheard by mentors, are:

> "They will not amount to anything, they will end up in jail," (Mentor: Cynthia).
> "Give them a few more years and they won't be giving anyone trouble except the prison guards," (Mentor: Derek).
> "Soon they will grow up to be thugs and drug dealers," (Mentor: Warren).
> "At the rate they are going, many will become mothers before they are fifteen," (Mentor: Rhea).
> "We are just wasting time. Many are not going anywhere. They will just end up in the streets," (Mentor: Latoya).

Contributing to the exacerbation of low self-esteem are the various negative labels placed on these youths, labels such as *kids from the projects*, *ADHD* students, *slow learners* or some fancier phrase as *academically challenged*. Regarding the ADHD (previously ADD) label, Hartman (1988:28) observed:

> ...even the labeling of a person with the term "Attention Deficit Disorder" is a form of wounding. It's an instant stigma...
>
> While this labeling may not be the first wounding that ADD children and adults experience in life, it is often one of the most severe, particularly for kids. Many a teenager has related to me that the pain and humiliation she or he experienced years earlier when first made to wear the ADD label for teachers and peers to see.

Given the negative consequences of labeling, building self-esteem becomes an integral component of the mentoring activity, and must be interwoven into the tutoring activity in order for learning to take place. The simultaneity of tutoring and building confidence and self esteem requires patience and creativity which mentors must constantly be aware of in order to be effective. The example of April and Mich helps to illustrate the simultaneity in tutoring and building self-esteem.

Helping Mich With His Self Confidence While Teaching Him To Read

When I went to the school, I was assigned to mentor Mich. Mich is a seven-year-old African American male with bright eyes, but a sad face. He looked like a child who was carrying a burden on his small shoulders, and hurting inside. Seeing how he stood there, when his teacher introduced him brought about some sadness in me. Just there and then, I decided I was going to help him as much as I can. As I talked to Mich, he did not say much. Many of my questions were left unanswered. I then asked him to read his book for me. Mich tried, but he could not sound the words, so I decided to teach him the alphabet. Very quickly, I realized that Mich was unsure of himself. He could not tell me a "D" from a "P". I was sad and disappointed at the same time. To encourage Mich, and build his self confidence, I said to him, "Mich you know what, I think you *tricking* me. You don't want me to see how smart you are. That's the truth isn't it?" When I said this he smiled. As I was ready to leave that morning, Mich whispered to me, "Do you think I really smart fo truth?"
"Yes," I responded, and then added. "You think you could fool me eh! Mich?" I then gave him a hug and told him I will be back...

Last week Mich couldn't tell me a "D" from a "P", but this week he has improved. He could recite the alphabet from A to Z, but he has difficulty differentiating between an S and X. He knew the different sounds of the letters but could not identify them. I could see that his little mind was working, and that he was beginning to withdraw because of his difficulties. I quickly told him that I knew he could do it and asked him to copy from the page I had written. I also told him to sound the letters out while he is copying them. Since I had done this before, he understood and followed my example. When he was finished, I told him how proud I was of him. Then, I said, "Come give me two hugs now, one for doing well, and one for you to keep on studying your alphabet." When I said this, Mich leaped forward and hugged me tightly twice...

Today, I was very impressed to see that Mich had done what I asked him, which is to study his words on his own. When I came into the classroom, he was glad to see me because he knew I would be proud. It seemed to me that he had been studying since the time I had left him the week before. He was right on task, and he had no problem with the pronunciation of his words. He pulled out his book and came directly over to me to read the whole story without

asking for help. Mich was proud of his accomplishment and asked: "Did I do good Ms. April?"
"Oh, sure you have Mich, you are my little hero," I responded with a smile. He then said he had been studying all week long to prepare for reading this week. I was very happy to see Mich had finally gotten the courage and strength to believe in himself. To reassure him, I started calling him on the phone and asked him to read to me. Each time he read well, I told him what a great job he was doing…

Today Mich seemed troubled. He thought I would be upset with him, because he didn't know the words to the next story we had planned the week before, to study for today. When I came in, he had a sad look on his face. I asked him what was wrong. He did not respond except to look down at the table, and bite on his fingernails. I begged him to get the book we had planned to read, and read me the stories. He hesitated for a moment, but eventually got up and brought the book. He opened it to the story *The Magic Boat.* To my surprise, he had difficulties pronouncing the words. I was truly disappointed. Sensing that something was wrong in his little world, I tried not to show my disappointment. Instead of teaching him the words, I said: "Mich, do you trust me?"
"Yes Ma'am," he responded.
"Mich, please don't call me Ma'am. You know my name, don't you?"
"Yes Maa.. Ms. April," he responded quietly.
"Do you think I love you?" I asked.
"Yes Ms. April," he replied, this time looking down at the floor.
"Mich, if you know that I love you, why can't you tell me what's wrong?"
Almost in a whisper, he said: "I have to keep my little brother evrday, and I git hollad if he did wrong. I didn have no time to study my words."
Listening to Mich, my heart went out to him. I reassured him over and over that I was not angry with him, and that I know if he had the time he would have studied his words. Remembering what was said in an earlier mentoring classroom discussion, I gave Mich some index cards and showed him how to write the words down. I explained that he could keep the cards in his pocket and study them while he takes care of his little brother. Mich was so happy he could learn his words while taking care of his brother, he phoned me to tell me he knew all his words and that he did not "git hollad at, not one time." I laughed so hard when he said this, my tears rolled down my cheeks (Mentor: April).

April encountered less and less difficulties and continued to work with Mich until she graduated. She wrote: "Mich has finally gained confidence in himself and he sees that he can do whatever he puts his mind to doing. I am proud to say that I played a part in helping him to become a better person and reader. I know I will miss him but I plan to stay in touch."

A mentee's low self esteem may not always be because of learning difficulties. The following case shows that low self-esteem could be tied to one's physical appearance which in turn impacts self perception, social relationships and academic progress. Here is how one mentor helped a mentee to deal with her negative self-perception and low self- esteem, and positively turn her life around.

How Building A Mentee's Self Esteem Helped Her to Excel

> Shaun is one who can be described as an individual who reflects the essence of what is best described as decency, integrity and generosity – values that most believe are absent in her generation. Shaun is an individual bestowed with the natural capacity for academic success and has utilized these talents to not only help herself perform in the academic arena, but to assist others in gaining academic success for themselves as well.
>
> During her middle school years, Shaun gained a noticeable amount of weight. Like any child during that age with a shift in body structure, her self-confidence was hit with a bitter blow-- not only because of her weight gain but because her peers, who were envious of her amazing natural aptitude, made fun of her as a result of the weight gain. However, unlike others in her same situation, Shaun had a mentor, Bridgette, who aided Shaun in cultivating the view point of not allowing this new challenge of weight gain to hinder her from being successful. She endured the challenges of her new body and despite the difficulties of living in a small town with limited resources to assist with health and fitness, during her eighth grade year, Shaun with Bridgette's support decided to do something about it. Along with the support of a neighborhood center's members and club staff, Shaun not only participated in physical activities at the local Boys & Girls

Club site, but also succeeded in making the cheering squad of her middle school.

Starting her membership during her primary years, Shaun is a seasoned member and leader in the organization. During a time when others of her age group celebrate youth in the traditional manner of parties and unpredictable rebellious acts, Shaun spends her high school years focused on participating in activities that make a difference in her school, community and have a positive impact on the center's members as a whole. She is the choreographer, a lead dancer and one of the originators of the center's jazz and hip-hop dance team Alpha Nu. Shaun tried out for the high school competitive cheerleading squad after her weight loss, and has been a member since her freshman year.

Though these achievements highlight the personal accomplishments of Shaun, those acts that specifically touched the lives of her fellow club members speak even more of her character. Uncommon of many high school level individuals, she spent a portion of her summer as a mentor for children between grade levels five through eight. In addition, Shaun seeing the need for the academic aid of her fellow peers (passing the torch has been achieved – the mentee becomes the mentor), put her own academics aside and asserted herself as a student tutor during the at her local high school. With this selfless act, she aided in helping students to succeed in areas of academic success that ordinarily would not see this success without the additional aid.

While matriculating through her high school career, Shaun maintained a 3.9 un-weighted grade point average with her regular AP high school courses, and a 4.0 grade point average in her dual enrolled college courses that she took while attending her local junior college and university. In addition to maintaining these high academic standards, she also remained an active member of the National Honor Society, Beta Club, and numerous other civic organizations.

Following graduation, Shaun plans to attend college and will enter the university level with enough earned credits to be classified as a first Semester Junior at the age of eighteen (Danae: former JJRMDP mentor and current voluntary organization supervisor).

The case of Shaun serves an excellent example of what a mentee can accomplish when one's self-esteem and self-confidence are restored.

Teaching Critical Thinking:

One of the most fundamental problems faced by mentor-tutors is to be able to teach mentees to think critically, even at a rudimentary level. Even though very much a part of the public debate, critical thinking gets lost in the educational setting where schools are assessed and rewarded on the basis of students' performances on standardized tests. Since at-risk African American children do not perform well on standardized tests, they find themselves further stigmatized, their schools get penalized, and consequently their teachers become disillusioned within a short period of time. The end result is academic flight, a process whereby teachers leave, and middle-income parents transfer their children to better performing schools.

To alleviate their schools downward academic spiral, and improve students' pass rates, most teachers find it advantageous to teach to the standardized tests. This emphasis on pass rates at standardized tests encourages learning by way of rote-memorization and regurgitation. In so doing, critical thinking becomes undermined. Critical thinking involves going beyond rote-memorization and regurgitation, by requiring mentees to use the mind and brain visually and spatially, when trying to solve a problem or understanding a statement. However, instead of encouraging critical thinking, mentors find themselves conforming to the rote-memorization and regurgitation method inherent in the school system. This is how some mentors explain the system of learning process.

> The only reason Freda reads the way she does is because her teacher makes her do things over and over again. Today, we had the students go over again the practice test for the up coming statewide exam, (Mentor: Kasey).
>
> The teacher gave me a packet to go over with the kids. She said to work with them until they caught on, so I had to explain the problem over and over again to each individual child until they understood, (Mentor: Talia).

> Each student again has a copy of the Test Ready booklet for Reading. I inquired from Rudy [mentee] what exam was the class preparing for, and he replied that they will be tested in Reading soon. Seeing they were going over the same thing again and again, I borrowed a booklet and Rudy and I began practicing for his reading exam, (Mentor: Sabrina).

The emphasis on memorization did not deter some mentors from getting their mentees to think critically. In the following example Anthony explained how he got his mentee Wynn to pronounce words by association.

> Today the emphasis was on reading. I had noticed that whenever students read, they did so as if they rehearsed the lesson. Whenever they stumbled upon the pronunciation of a word, the teacher pronounced the word for them... As I listened to Wynn read, he would stumble on certain words. As the words became more difficult, he became agitated. Instead of giving him the pronunciation as his teacher had done, I decided I would teach him how to figure it out for himself. First the word was *provide*. I asked Wynn what rhymes with *hide* but starts with a *v*. He quickly gave me the correct answer. When he came to the prefix *pro*, he kept pronouncing it *pra* several times. Knowing that he loves basketball and talks a lot about the game, I asked him about his favorite player Michael Jordan. I asked him if he thinks Michael is a *little league* player or a *professional* player, emphasizing the words. He said professional. I then wrote down professional on the paper and asked him to pronounce it twice. After he did so, I asked him to look at *provide* and *professional* and pronounce *provide*. After whispering to himself a few seconds, he said, "I get it, I get it, provide." He pronounced the word correctly and smiled. We did several more words to build his confidence... (Mentor: Anthony).

In this next example, mentor Davis explains the method he used in teaching Jamal, his mentee, how to write a paragraph. Aware that Jamal dislikes writing, Davis encouraged him to orally explain what he would like to say before asking him put his thoughts down on paper. This is how Davis explains his technique.

> I know that Jamal hates to write. Usually, he writes a paragraph, and it never makes sense. Then his teacher corrects his mistakes, and tells Jamal to rewrite it. I decided to get Jamal to write his

> paper to make sense, and with little mistakes as possible… It took a while but he did. This is how I did it. I first let him tell me what he wanted to write about. Then I asked him to tell it to me again… First, he was angry, but he quieted down when I told him I want to show my friends what a smart guy he is. … I then asked him to tell me again, but to think hard on what he wanted to say and, to count the number of things he wanted to write about… Because the story changed a little, we talked about the things he left out and those that he added. I then asked him to tell me the story one more time, and to think even harder about what he really wanted to write about. He did so reluctantly. When he wrote his paper, it made sense; and he did not make so many mistakes. I congratulated him and he was very happy. The funny part is that once he realized he could write a story, he wanted to read it to me over and over (Mentor: Davis).

Some mentors use their mentees lived experiences to get them to think critically. For example, when Freddie found out that his mentee constantly complained about drugs and how if affects his mother, Freddie explained that he felt very sorry for the nine year old. He then seized upon an opportunity to question him more about his feelings and the things he could do about it.

> I asked Mickey what he wanted to see happen to the drug dealers in his neighborhood. He said he wanted them dead. I asked him what happens to a person who kills another person, he said, "Go to jail."
> I asked him if he would like to go to jail for killing a drug dealer, he said, "No."
> I then asked him what else he can do to get rid of the drug dealers. After thinking about it for a short while he said, "I am going to be a policeman first, then kill the drug dealers."
> When I explained to him that a policeman can lose his job and may even go to jail for killing someone, he looked at me as if he was confused. I then explained to him that as a policeman, he can arrest the drug dealers and put them in jail. Mickey quickly said that the drugs dealers will get a rich lawyer to get them out of jail. "Can you do anything to stop the rich lawyer from getting the drug dealers out of jail?" I asked. He said, "No." I asked him to think harder but after trying to think for a few seconds he shook his head "No." To get him to think a little harder, I asked him who can put away people in prison for a long time. He thought about it for a while and then said, "A judge." After thinking about it for a few seconds more Mikey said, "Now I get it, I can be a judge, and when the policeman arrest the drug dealers I can put them in jail for a

> long, long time." I then told Mickey he can be anything he wants to be if he studied hard. He looked at me with a big smile on his face, (Mentor: Freddie).

The above examples serve to illustrate how some mentors encouraged their mentees to think critically. They challenged their mentees to use their imaginations and their minds to arrive at better answers or solutions to their problems. Instead of providing their mentees with answers, the mentors provided these youths with bits and pieces of information, and then steered or nudged them into trying harder.

Addressing Sensitive Issues:

Not uncommon in the mentoring process are situations in which the mentor must seek to address mentees personal hygiene problems. Pushed to the brink of existence as a result of their poverty, their inability to cope, or lack of parenting skills, some low-income parents react by neglecting their children. While some seek refuge in drugs and alcohol, others try to cope with the deteriorating economic conditions by denying themselves and their children some very basic amenities such as clean clothes, soap, toothpaste etc. These parental actions leave many children to fend and care for themselves. Unable or ill equipped to adequately care for themselves; many of the neglected children experience problems of personal hygiene. Given its sensitivity, mentors often find themselves threading cautiously when seeking to address mentees personal hygiene problems.

For example, shortly after being assigned his mentee, Trevor realized that the youth had a very strong body odor. At first, he ignored the scent hoping that on his next visit his mentee would have solved the problem, but this was not the case. On the second visit, a frustrated Trevor cuts short his tutoring, telling the mentee that he would see him the following week. Again, Trevor had hoped that the problem would be solved but came away disappointed. After Trevor and I discussed the issue, Trevor seemed to have solved the problem. Trevor explained:

> I never thought a kid could smell so bad, but when Darion told me he never had a shower it made sense, but I was still shocked. He told me that they didn't have a shower at home. Some times,

> Darion takes a bath by pouring water over himself from a bucket, but never uses any soap. He then wears the same clothes, which get washed on weekends. On Saturday, with his mother's permission, I took Darion to the mall. I bought a tee shirt for myself, and then asked him to pick up a tee shirt and a pair of shorts for himself. He was reluctant but when I told him I will pay for them, he picked out one of each. I then took Darion to my apartment where we made sandwiches. After eating, I told him I was going to take a shower. After I did, I put on my new tee shirt. I then asked him if I smelled clean. He said, "Yes". I told him it is because I used soap. Since Darion had told me he did not like to shower, I asked him if he wanted to put on his new clothes and smell like me, he didn't answer. I then told him that I was going to the movies and would have taken him with me, but since he has on dirty clothes I can't, so I have to take him home. At this point Darion begged me to take him to the movies. I told him that the only way he could go with me is if he took a shower, and used soap. He agreed.
> Within two minutes he was out of the shower, so I sent him back. This time he took a little longer, even singing in the shower. When he was all dressed up, I told him he smelled nice and clean. This made him smile... Before I took Darion back home that night, I gave him some soap and tooth paste and told him if he uses them everyday, I will take him out on weekends... Now, when I go to mentor Darion he always asks me if he smells clean because he uses soap when he bathes, (Mentor: Trevor).

Sometimes, in the process of mentoring, a mentor may have to decide whether or not to address sensitive biological changes. Especially in working with young female mentees, mentors have found themselves faced with the difficult task of explaining the coming of age, and the importance of proper care. Because of the sensitive nature of the issue, and the potential psychosocial risk it poses, mentors may have to exercise caution as well as good judgment. In the following example Danielle's explains how she addressed the issue of biological change with her thirteen-year-old mentee.

> One of the most difficult aspects of my mentoring thus far was to explain to Kesha the coming of age, and biological changes in young girls. When I visited her yesterday, she kept complaining about stomachaches. Thinking that she didn't want to work on her Math, as we had previously agreed, I asked somewhat bluntly at first: "What is wrong with you? Do you want me to take her to the clinic?" She quickly responded, "NO" and remained quiet for a

> while. From time to time, she would wrap her hands around herself as if to console herself. I then persuaded her into telling me her problem. Trying not to embarrass her, I asked her if anyone explained to her "things" about biological changes in girls. She said the nurse at her school did, but that she did not understand much of what was said, or what to do about it. When I asked her if she spoke to her mom, she said she was afraid. She also said that since her mother never explained anything to her, she was not sure her mother can address her problem. I told her I will accompany her to talk to her mom but she refused.
>
> Knowing the sensitivity of the issue, and how some parents can react, I must admit, I was a little nervous, so I called her mom and obtained her permission... Initially, I did not know how to begin the conservation. However, recalling what my mother, a schoolteacher, taught me, I explained slowly to Kesha step by step what she needed to do to address her problem, and the proper way to take care of herself. I paused regularly to make sure she understood what I was saying. I remember emphasizing to her the health risks and benefits of proper care, just as my mom did to me. I also emphasized that she needed to speak personally with the nurse at school, and that I would be happy to accompany her if she so desires...
>
> On my way driving home that evening, I kept wondering if I did the right thing. At one point, I realized I was talking to myself, asking: "I wonder how many little girls are out there feeling frightened and all alone, because of the pains of coming of age and not sure what to do about it?"
>
> Before I went to bed, I called my mom to thank her for what she did for me, (Mentor: Danielle).

Because of the sensitive nature of some problems faced by mentees, most mentors will likely ignore them. Unlike Danille, mentors may find that sensitive personal issues create discomforts for both mentors and mentees. One suggestion is to bring the problem to the attention of the parents, or the school personnel. In cases where the mother may be inadequately prepared to address the problems, mentors could follow the approach Danielle took, and seek permission from the parent, or have the parent present when addressing sensitive issues.

THINGS TO REMEMBER

- Tutoring at-risk youths in reading and math is only one aspect of mentoring. If tutoring is to succeed, it must be accompanied by culturally relevant materials, and an understanding of mentees learning difficulties.
- In the process of instructional mentorship, mentors must integrate the building of self confidence and self esteem into the tutoring activity.
- In assisting mentees with their self confidence and self esteem, mentors must be sensitive to negative factors and stereotypic labels that contribute to the lack of self confidence and low self-esteem.
- Effective instructional mentorship involves going beyond rote-memorization and regurgitation by teaching mentees to think critically.
- Critical thinking necessitates the incorporation of mentees social-cultural histories into the learning process in order to stimulate them to use their minds and brains visually and spatially when trying to solve a problem or understand a statement.

DISCUSSION QUESTIONS AND EXERCISES

1. For the purposes of mentoring, why is it necessary to understand discriminatory practices as it relates to the education of Africans Americans?

2. In what ways do schools and teachers serve to diminish or destroy at-risk African American youths' confidence and self esteem? Explain.

3. Discuss how April was able to help Mitch with his self-confidence. What would you have done differently? Explain.

4. How would you assess whether or not your mentee is being taught to think critically?

5. Anthony, Davis and Freddie used different methods to assist their mentees to think critically: Do you agree or disagree with their approaches? Explain.

6. In mentoring you may be called upon to assist your mentee with sensitive personal issues: What are some of things you would consider before undertaking such a task?

7. Trevor and Danille took different approaches in addressing the sensitive issues of their mentees. Assess the strengths and weaknesses of their approaches.

CHAPTER 10

In Mentoring At-risk Youths, it is Sometimes Necessary for Mentors to Have Some Familiarity With the Juvenile Justice System

African American Youths and the Juvenile Justice System:

African American youths today are arrested and brought before the Juvenile Justice System at an alarming rate more than any other ethnic group in the society. Because of this, *some volunteers may find themselves mentoring youths who are already in the Juvenile Justice System or who, later in the mentoring process, become entangled in the system.* Already the victims of poverty, these youths must face a justice system that is increasingly punishment oriented. In their book *Juvenile Justice in America,* Bartollas and Miller (2001:426), noted that: "The juvenile justice system has too long been a disposal unit for the children of the poor. The lack of social justice for the poor and minority groups is a grave indictment of our society. At the same time that the heavy-handed ministrations of the state have harshly processed the poor, the justice system has worked very hard at saving the 'saved'-the middle class youths who have committed minor offenses."

Perceptions of Authority:

Bortallas and Miller's comments ring true for African American youths, many of whom have experienced unequal treatment under the Juvenile Justice System. Given the unequal distribution of justice, many African American youths, as young as seven years, find themselves face to face with a justice system that they have no understanding of, or how it impacts their lives. Too young to understand the consequences of their own misbehaviors, these youths are processed, and brought before courts *without an understanding of the authority* of the judge. **Many find it difficult to grasp society's relations of power and authority, because they were socialized by parents and adult relatives who themselves do not understand such relations.** Furthermore, many of these adults may have developed a one-dimensional punitive view of legal authority, as a result of prejudices and discrimination, and hence refrain from discussing it with their youthful children. T. Howard captures the contradictions in relations of authority well when she observed the trial of the eleven-year whom she was recently assigned to mentor.

Kim Talks Back to the Judge:

> Today, I went to court with Kim and her grandmother. When the judge called Kim to the stand, she did not move from her seat, but kept looking at her grandmother. When her name was announced a second time, a guard came over to her and told her to move to the front of the court. She again looked at her grandmother, who then moved over to her and directed her to the front of the court. After the judge read her charges of shoplifting and resisting arrest, Kim turned to look at her grandmother again. At this point, the judge asked Kim's grandmother to stand by her. As the judge continued the trial, Kim started to play with her braids and seemed not to pay any attention to the judge. After talking for a few seconds, the judge stopped his explanation of the charges and told Kim to stop playing with her braids, and pay attention to him. Kim did not listen to the judge, and kept on playing with her braids. The judge stopped a second time, and firmly told Kim to stop playing with her braids and listen. Kim then pointed to the judge, and with body language and all, as she moved her head from side to side, she pointed to the judge and then to herself and said, "You talking to me mister?" This shocked the entire court. The judge then called upon the bailiff to remove her from the court and "talk some sense into her." As she was being carried into the next room, Kim started to cry and turned back to call on her grandmother to get her.
>
> Later, Kim's grandmother told me that she raised Kim since she was a baby because Kim's mom was and addict and did not take care of Kim very well. She said she tried to shield Kim from the bad influences of her mother and her friends, and always taught her to do what was right. She did not know why Kim stole from the store… It appears to me that Kim did not listen to anyone except her grandmother. It seemed clear that she did not understand the court's proceedings or the authority of the judge.

The case of Kim is not unusual. Many at-risk youths today regularly have difficulties differentiating between formal and informal authority because of the way they were socialized or introduced to these forms of authority.

Often this leads to confusion and indifference as we will see in the section that follows.

A Day in Juvenile Court:

Today, an increasing number of youths lead lives that bring them into contact with the juvenile justice system. This has led many parents to seek out assistance from mentors that goes beyond tutoring academic subjects. Called upon to give moral support or provide testimonies of their services to at-risk youths, mentors are becoming increasingly involved in the juvenile justice process. For mentors who never before experienced the workings of the judicial system, the actual real life proceedings of the court, especially the manner in which justice is dispensed, can be a harrowing experience. The following courtroom drama captures the case of a fourteen years old juvenile, and the reactions of some mentors who attended the day's proceedings. These mentors had agreed to accompany one of their colleagues, Martha, whose mentee was on trial for shoplifting and resisting arrest. Since neither Martha nor her mentor colleagues had attended court before, they asked me to accompany them. What the mentors witnessed in court that day seemed to shock them, especially the sentencing of the youth whom the guards took into custody before his mother could reach over and hug him. This is what occurred.

Not Enough Time For a Hug

> Suddenly, the buzzing courtroom became quiet as the presiding judge began his sentencing of the 14 years old delinquent. Just a few minutes before, the youth stood slouched beside his mother as the judge asked repeatedly whether he understood the proceedings of the court. Each time the judge asked the question, the youth answered, "Yes". As if to ascertain that the youth and his mother understood the court's proceedings the judge then asked, "Can you both read?" The mother and son responded in unison, "Yes Sir." Upon hearing this reply and indicating that that he had examined all the evidence before him, the judge said: "You are hereby sentenced to sixty-days to be served at a level six facility."
>
> The youth, who had not changed his posture before the sentencing, now stood erect. Almost immediately, an officer of the court sprang forward, handcuffed the youth, emptied his

pockets and took him by his arm ready to lead him out of the courtroom. Both mother and son stood momentarily transfixed. They stared at each other with bewildered expressions on their faces. Their body languages seemed to convey messages of doubt and despair. As the officer led the youth toward the court's exit, the mother made an attempt to reach out for him. Her right hand came up halfway only to fall back at her side as she realized she could not reach her son. With every step he took towards the exit, the youth tried to twist from the grips of the court officer to glance back at his mother who still stood motionless in the middle of the courtroom. In their quiet stares, they appeared to be asking what has just taken place. Lost from each other's view by a closed exit door, the mother turned and walked out of the courtroom.

From behind me someone tugged at my coat sleeve. It was one of Juvenile Justice Role Model Development Program (JJRMDP) mentors who, along with a few other mentors, had accompanied us to the Juvenile Court. "What happened?" she asked. "He was sentenced to a correctional facility," I replied. "I know that," she said. "But why didn't his mother get to hug him?" "She probably was not prepared for such a sentence, or felt she would have a few moments with him before he was taken into custody." Just then, a parent who had previously contacted the JJRMDP for help with her son joined in the conversation. She explained that many of the problem youths and their parents truly do not understand the court's proceedings. "They are embarrassed to say that they do not understand the court system. These parents need lots and lots of help." I responded that I also have a difficult time following the proceedings, given all the legalese and the rapid pace of the hearings. She replied almost instantly, "If it is hard for you, what about people like us."

As we drove back to campus that day, the JJRMDP mentors who accompanied me reflected on the day's happenings. "I can't believe so many young kids are in trouble these days," one mentor said. To this comment another responded, "Did you see the little one in chains, he couldn't be more than seven, or eight years old. It is truly sad. A kid so young [pause]. I would take a bet he didn't know what was going on in the courtroom."

Commenting on their day in juvenile court, students noted the sadness in the faces of the mother and son as they heard the sentence. "Don't you think that lady whose son was sentenced to

> sixty-days would have liked some support from someone?" a mentor turned to me and asked. This question evoked a vivid recall of the expression on the mother's face as she walked out of the courtroom. She was biting on her lower lip in her efforts to hold back her tears. No sooner had she exited the courtroom, and with her back towards me, she raised her head to the sky and with the back of her right hand she wiped her eyes. Realizing that in my moment of reflection I had forgotten to respond to the mentor's question, I said quietly as an afterthought, "I guess." No one seemed to hear my response. It appeared that they too were thinking of the mother and her son and the hug that sentencing did not permit.

The above illustration helps to draw attention to some of the difficulties many poor parents and their youthful children encounter in the juvenile court system. Poorly educated themselves, and without any legal representation, they must negotiate their way through a complex court system. Called upon by such parents for support, many mentors also find themselves equally lost in the maze of the juvenile justice system. Despite instruction and training about the juvenile justice system many mentors regularly admit their difficulties in following and understanding the actual proceedings of the court. "Too much legalese," many mentors often acknowledged. "If I can't follow what is going on in court and I am taking courses in criminal justice, what about the parents and the kids who don't even have a tenth grade education?" William asked. Instead of taking it upon themselves to explain to mentees' parents the workings of the juvenile justice system, mentors may find it more expedient to serve as the link between parents, law enforcement agencies and the juvenile justice system by exploring ways to facilitate communication and information flow that would minimize misconceptions and indifferences among all these entities. Mentors could also seek out information and assistance on prevention, intervention, rehabilitation and other essential services that would be helpful to their mentees and parents.

Legalese is a Foreign Language:

A common difficulty for many African American parents is the lack of understanding, and often misunderstanding of, the legal language of the juvenile justice system. Simply put, for many African American parents, legalese is a foreign language. "The legal language of the juvenile justice system was not written for poor African Americans to understand. It is meant to punish them," said mentor Danae. This comment finds support in Arrigo's observations that: "Linguistic formulations…have power. Legal language is not a mere tool, a neutral vehicle, because it is a means of classifying, controlling, and sanctioning citizens. Power sanctions legal language and expresses the interests of governmental agents of control, even when it remains an "open text," subject to interpretation," (Arrigo, 1999:132).

For many poor African Americans, the interpretation of legal language is often quite baffling. In cases involving mentees, parents and mentees regularly turn to mentors for assistance in explaining the legal process. For many mentors, such requests add to the burden of mentoring. Since many disadvantaged Africans view the legal system as discriminatory and arbitrarily punitive, request for assistance could result in parent-mentor conflict. Such was the case of Iman.

Contempt is Not Just Another Fancy Word:

> Assigned to mentor Cedric after Cedric's fifteen-year-old brother was arrested for the third time, Iman accompanied Cedric's family to court. During the hearing, the judge cautioned Cedric's mother who failed to appear at the previous trial date, that if she didn't appear in court with her son, she would be charged with "contempt." According to Iman, Cedric's mother explained to the judge that she finds it difficult to attend court because she is a single mom with two sons, and holding on to a low paying job that grants no time off except in cases of illness. She also explained that she did not have a car, and must rely on public transportation to go everywhere. While the judge dismissed her explanation, Cedric's mom felt that she told the truth, and that the judge must accept the truth. She believed that she did not have to accompany her son to court. Iman tried to explain to her that while she told the truth about her situation, she has to attend court otherwise she will be cited for contempt of court. She disagreed and chided Iman for his use of "his fancy words."

On the day of the trial, Iman asked me to accompany Cedric and his brother to court. Not knowing what had occurred on the previous trial date, I took Iman, Cedric and his brother to court. When the clerk announced Cedric brother's case, the judged inquired about the absence of his mother. After a momentary pause, the judge declared to Cedric's brother that if his mother does not appear in court within the next half an hour, she would be charged with contempt of court. Upon hearing this, Iman, Cedric and I rushed to get Cedric's mother. When we arrived at her home at about 10:30 a.m., she was still in her sleeping clothes. Cedric explained to her the judge's intent, and insisted that she attend court. Hurriedly dressed, and with curlers in her hair, we rushed to court in time for her son's case. After being admonished by the court, the judge sentenced her son to community service with probation, and cautioned her never to be late again.

Driving her home after court that day, I explained to Cedric's mom the meaning of "contempt of court," but she seemed to pay no heed. When we arrived at her home, she got out of the car and slammed the door shut without saying a word. About a month later, standing in front of my office, I saw a lady dashing across the road against the traffic, waving her hand and calling. It was Cedric's mom. I had hardly recognized her when she hugged me and thanked me for being there for her and her son. She hurriedly explained her struggles as a single parent, and the confusion and depression brought on by the juvenile justice system. She volunteered to share her story with all the mothers in our program. She also happily announced that both her sons are doing well and that they still laugh at her for going to court with curlers in her hair.

The experience with Cedric's mother made me realize how angry and confused parents can become when their loved ones, at a young age, must face the realities of a justice system that they do not, and perhaps, will never understand.

THINGS TO REMEMBER

- Many at-risk youths in need of mentoring services today are already in the Juvenile Justice System, and too young to understand the consequences of their own behavior and how the legal system affects their lives.
- A mentor is likely to be of greater assistance to a delinquent mentee is he/she seeks out ways to address the mentee's legal concerns instead of ignoring these, or pretending that they don't exist.
- At-risk youths and their parents often have difficulties in grasping society's relations of power and authority. They are regularly confused about the power and authority courts and judges have over their lives.
- It is not uncommon for at-risks youths to believe that the only people with power and authority over their lives are their parents and grandparents.
- Many adults who have raised at-risk youths have developed, or experienced a one-dimensional punitive view of legal authority as a result of prejudices and discrimination. Given such experience or view, they usually refrain from discussing the legal system with their youthful children.
- The legal proceedings and language of juvenile courts are not conducted and delivered with parents and at-risk youths' level of understanding and apprehension in mind.

DISCUSSION QUESTIONS AND EXERCISES

1. How would you assist your mentee in understanding the different types of power and authority in society?

2. Supposing you were Kim's mentee, how would you explain to her the authority the judge has over her?

3. Spend a day in juvenile court and record your observations. How you're your observations compare with that of the JJRMDP students as reported in "not Enough Time For a Hug?"

4. What would you do if you were asked to explain the legal language of the court to your mentee and his/her parents? Explain.

5. The parents of many at-risk youths are often confused and angry about the realities of the juvenile justice system. In your role as mentor, how would you assist them? Explain?

CHAPTER 11

Mentoring Means Working Against the Influences of the Material Culture, and Immediate Gratification in Order to Promote Deferred Gratification

Material Culture and Immediate Gratification:

By the time an at-risk African American youth comes in contact with a mentor, his psyche has already been penetrated and programmed for immediate gratification through material consumption. From food, to toys, to clothes, from little burgers, to big burgers, the material culture transforms the little consumers into bigger consumers, with no emphasis on, or concern for deferred gratification. Since mentoring provides mentees something of value in the long term, **mentors must constantly seek to minimize the influences of the material culture and its emphasis on immediate gratification.**

Contemporary culture glamorizes material consumption and extols the acquisition of newer and more sophisticated products that seem to create endless needs in all of us. One only has to turn on the television, open the pages of the newspapers and magazines, or scan the internet to see the multitude of products advertised each day that promise to make our lives happier if we acquire them. As corporations design new products or improve on old ones, we seem to vie with each other for the acquisition of "the state of the art" products as if these are testimonies of our self worth, our successes. Today, the new forms of commodity production and consumerism have penetrated all socio-economic layers of society and impacted the core existence of even the very young. In explaining the interrelationship between the new mode of commodity production and consumption, and how its impact young African Americans Kitwana (2002:9), states:

> Today more and more Black youth are turning to rap music, music videos, designer clothing, popular Black films, and television programs for values and identity. One can find faces, bodies, attitudes and language of Black youth attached to slick

> advertisements that sell what has become global products, whether its Coca-Cola and Pepsi, Reebok and Nike sneakers…
> Working diligently behind the scene and toward the bottom line are the multinational corporations that produce, distribute, and shape these images. That Black youth in New Orleans, Louisiana, and Champaign, Illinois, for example, share similar dress styles, colloquialisms, and body language with urban kids from Los Angeles, Chicago, and New York City, is not coincidental.

Kunjufu (2002) also noted that African Americans are obsessed with designer labels and immediate gratification even when they profess to be price conscious. To catch a glimpse of the influence of material culture on young mentees, let us turn to Arriale and her mentor Erica as an example.

My Elementary School Mentee And Material Consumption :

> After walking through the community center, I finally chose where I wanted to mentor that afternoon. I walked past the entertainment room to the playground outside, and finally set my eyes on the baseball field upon the hill. As I ventured towards the hill, I noticed a group of kids sitting on the bleachers busy chitchatting about other kids. I broke up their conversation by introducing myself to the group. At first they were apprehensive, but as I learned in the mentoring book, I have to speak their language. So, I decided to ask them about music and dance moves… one person who stood out from the group was Erica. She wore a white T-shirt with black jeans and name brand shoes. A cell phone adorned the side of her belt. She was eating spicy Cheetos as she picked on the other kids sitting on the bleachers. She read my T-shirt that said "Miami" and immediately asked me if I was from there. I told her I was. She then asked me if they had nice clothes and if I ever met the stars, referring to television actors… Two boys who were sitting on the bleachers were Erica's brother and cousin. They each had cell phones. They were only in the fifth grade….
> Today was a shocking day for me. I walked into the community center and someone flew past me saying hello. I looked for a quick second and the person was gone… It was Erica, in miniskirt and a halter top, her hair was in a ponytail … her look was somewhat revealing for someone still in elementary school … She was the same ol' Erica. Rude talking, cell phone wearing, bully of the clique.

What Arriale was able to show in the above is that at-risk youths are not immune to material consumption which influences and impacts their lives at a very young age.

Consumption and Self Worth:

It is not uncommon for disadvantaged youths to be preoccupied with immediate gratification and material possessions, as if these add value to their self worth. If the acquisition of material products add to a person's self worth, then the corollary should also hold true. That is, the inability to acquire such products brings about a devaluation of self worth. Hill (1999:87-90) explains the issue of self worth this way: "Children's self-perceptions are ... influenced by the larger social environment as children learn to see and evaluate themselves from the perspectives and standards of the "generalized other," or the community... it has conventionally been held that racism, negative stereotypes have a corrosive effect on the self-esteem of black children." For the African American at-risk youths, their already devalued self worth suffers further by the inability to acquire even a modicum of material possessions.

Residing in poverty does not exclude at-risk youths from embracing the notion that the acquisition of material products serves to enhance one's social status. Status enhancing products such as Nikes and Air Jordans, FUBU clothing, cell phones, gold chains etc. have permeated every nook and cranny of the African American community, bestowing pride on the youths who possess them. So valued are some of these products that youths have resorted to stealing, cheating, peddling drugs and even injuring someone in order to obtain their prized articles (see Garbarino 2000). As Majors and Billson (1993:80) state: "Clothes help the black male attract attention and enhance his self image...Clothes can also contribute to violence and fighting, even death among black males." Majors and Billson went on to explain that African American youths perceive the acquisition of material possessions as an aspect of being "Cool," and that being "Cool" does not correlate with school and the and its promises of deferred gratification. This perception of schooling and deferred gratification is perhaps best captured in the following poem cited in Majors and Billson (1992:47-48):

I was Cool

They said the doors of opportunity were closing fast,
and all the signs said that the good times weren't going to last,
but that didn't bother me,
because I was cool.

My teachers kept trying to get me to learn read'n, writ'n and math,
talking about you need that stuff to make it down life's paths.
But I just looked at them, and laughed.
I said, "Ya'll might need to know that stuff, but not me, because
I'm cool."

Them teachers was always getting on my case, and I told them
I knew that it was because of my race.
They just couldn't deal with me,
because they were square,
and I was cool.

I use to be so clean everybody would stop and stare,
'cause I was looking good with my curl free on my hair.
Hey, if you've got it, you've got it,
and I knew I was cool and looking good.
I didn't learn nothing in school, but they still let me pass.

I was sho gett'n ova,
Even I was at the bottom of my class.
But they still let me graduate from high school.
I definitely got ova!

But you can do that when you're cool.
After grad-u-ation I got clean and went to look for me a job.
I knew I was going to make me some long bread, buy me a new
ride,
and stay clean and cool everyday!
I was definitely going to have everything my way!

But trying to read them job applications was far from a charm,
and I told the dude at the employment office I couldn't write too
good,
'cause I'd hurt my arm.

But the look on his face told me that he really didn't believe that,
and the dude wasn't hardly impressed by my bad new hat.

Well to make a long story short, I finally got me a job,
but I don't get much pay,
and from the way things look its always gonna be that way.
I didn't learn much in school,
and you sure don't get paid much when all you can do is be cool.

If I could go back to school I'd learn all I could,
and every time I talk to other brothers I tell them they should.
I realize now that my future's not too bright,
and without an education it's kinda hard to make things right.

You know now that I think about it,
maybe some of those teachers that I thought was getting on my
case,
were actually trying to help me in the education race.
It sure hurts when I realize that with my abilities,
I could have been anything that I wanted to be,
if I had applied myself in school.
But instead of learning all I could in school,
I spent most of my time,
sitting in the back of the room,
looking good,
and being cool.

The above poem clearly illustrates that educating a disadvantaged youth is preparing him/her for the future. However, unable to conceptualize the future in concrete terms, many youths resist their education preparation, only to regret through retrospection, as their adult circumstances force them to look backwards. **Similar to formal education, in mentoring, you are teaching at-risk African American youths deferred gratification. You are teaching, guiding, and counseling these youths to look past their present into the future; a future distorted by their current reality of residing in poverty** and the warped models of economic success that emerge out of it. Victims of poverty, many these youths find it impossible to see past their immediate circumstances. What they see as exemplars of success, by way of the adults from their neighborhoods, are drug dealers, hustlers and other deviants. To such circumstances Boyd and Allen (1996:xxv) provide the following explanation:

> That old, familiar, but relatively stable process of leaving home, acquiring a modicum of education, and then settling into a job demanding only minimum skills no longer exists. An unusually high dropout rate among African American male students coupled with a distressingly small number of employment opportunities has drastically changed this picture. A minimum wage job at some fast food outlet is about all the large pool of unskilled young Black men can hope for, and it is unrealistic to expect these jobs to compete with the lucrative lure of selling illegal drugs.

Given the negative adult models of success in many poor neighborhoods, mentors are likely to be seen as the exceptions to these community models. Mentors must therefore be alert to misrepresentations of success when attempting to inculcate in their mentees the value of deferred gratification.

THINGS TO REMEMBER

- Contemporary culture glorifies material consumption and the ownership and possession of *state of the art* products.
- By the time an at-risk youth comes into contact with a mentor, his psyche has already been penetrated and programmed to seek out immediate gratification; to value material things from clothing and jewelry to computer games and cell phones.
- For at-risk youths, deferred gratification is something unreal, an idea difficult to conceptualize since it does not bring happiness to their current lives or changes in their lived circumstances.
- Mentoring is likely to be frustrating when teaching at-risk youths the value of education (schooling) and its relation to deferred gratification.
- Despite the potential frustration, mentors, if they are to have a positive impact, cannot afford to ignore or overlook the influence of the material culture on the future lives of mentees.

DISCUSSION QUESTIONS AND EXERCISES

1. In what ways does our material culture influence the lives of many at-risk youths? Explain.

2. How would go about explaining deferred gratification to your mentee?

3. What would you do if your mentee is preoccupied with material consumption? Explain.

4. How is material consumption tied to at-risk youths self worth? Explain.

5. Read and discuss with your mentee the poem "I was Cool," then ask your mentee to explain what he/she has learned from it.

6. Why is it difficult for many at-risk youths to see beyond their own lived circumstances? How would you assist your mentee to look into the future? Explain.

CHAPTER 12

Being a Mentor, One Must Realize That an Individual's Lived Experiences Could be Shared But Cannot be Readily Transferred to Another:

The Lived Experience:

Many successful people seeking to become mentors to at-risk youths do so with the shared conviction that their lived experiences can be utilized to positively influence the lives of these youths. The general belief is that by sharing their lived experiences, they would be able to instill some of their awareness and knowledge in the minds of their mentees. **In the process of mentoring, mentors must keep in mind that the lived experiences can be shared and utilized to influence their mentees, but cannot be transferred from one individual to another.** Moreover, even when shared, there is no assurance that the lived experience will have the desired effect on the individual to whom it is targeted. We cannot change disadvantaged youths by telling them to change because we know change to be beneficial. Even parents, who have made mistakes in their youth, find that it is impossible to transfer their lived experiences unto their youthful children. This lesson came as a harsh reality to Jonetta Barras, who experienced strong resistance from her daughter as she tried to let her daughter understand the consequences of having a baby like she [Barras] did. Barras (2000:88) writes:

Although I understand it, this baby thing drives me crazy—maybe it takes me too deeply into the alcoves of my own past. I look for some reason for the obsession and conclude that the new boyfriend Afrika has found is encouraging her behavior. I am sure of it.

> Not long after he came, the altars began to be assembled. He seems a nice guy, but neither he nor she is ready for parent hood. I try to impress upon them the demands of children. Try to make sure that he understands there is someone who is going to protect her and that he cannot take advantage of the situation. I emphasize that she is going to make something of herself; she will not repeat the mistakes of her mother and her grandmother.
>
> But I have been talking to the wind.

Heeding Barras, and the multitude of other parents, mentors would not be easily dismayed if it happens that their shared experiences of coping with poverty, school, and other personal problems does not have the intended effects on their mentees.

Poverty A Harsh Teacher:

Poverty indeed is a harsh teacher, and not everyone perceives it the same way, nor is everyone affected by it in similar fashion. **No two experiences of the realities of poverty and hardships are the same**. It is erroneous to assume that poor at-risk youths share the same realities, and the same social constructs, as successful adults. Adults who never before experienced hunger are not likely to understand the pain and emotional mood swings of at-risk youths who suffer from hunger. **The lessons of poverty and its consequences are varied and quite often difficult to translate in meaningful ways.** Despite this awareness, mentors can become frustrated when their explanations of their lived experiences and how they climbed out of poverty are not heeded or followed by their mentees. The tendency is to think that: "I have so much to offer, if only my mentee would listen." To the mentee, however, a mentor's explanation of climbing out of poverty or coping with difficulties may seem irrelevant to his/her lived circumstances. It is therefore not unusual for mentors to be rejected by their mentees even when they share similar experiences. This is evidenced in the relationship between Nesha and her fifteen-year-old single-parent mentee.

Sharing Experiences Proved Difficult

> When I first met Mia, I was convinced I would be able to help her. She happens to be in the same situation I was in, when I was her age, young, with one child and a tenth grade education. I was scared, depressed and unsure about me and my child's future. I knew I could depend on my parents for assistance, but for how long? At first, I didn't think a child needed much of anything, but as my daughter grew, it became increasingly difficult for both of us. My mom helped with her while I tried to stay in school, but my schooling began to suffer as my daughter became irritable or ill, and I stayed home more and more to take care of her. Missing classes, my grades began to suffer and so I had to work harder

> which was very frustrating. After much struggling and lots of anger and tears, I finally finished high school and am now in college…
>
> To help Mia with her problems, I tried to let her know that I understand her difficulties. I explained to her the difficulties I went through and what I did to overcome my problems. After explaining the difficulties I had as a young mother, it seemed as if Mia understood. Her grades improved for a while and then began to drop again. One day when she became really frustrated, I tried to comfort her. I told her I understood her problems, but she quickly turned on me and said, "No you don't, leave me alone." I was hurt and left…
>
> Shortly after this incident, Mia dropped out of school (Mentor: Nesha).

Mentors should not presume that because they share similar backgrounds with their mentees they are destined to success. At-risk youths differ in many ways, including personality and temperament. Similar family backgrounds and a common ethnicity may help in establishing rapport and may hasten the bonding between mentor and mentee but these characteristics do not guarantee success. Mentors may try to let their mentees know that they too suffered in their youth, and offer suggestions of how to cope, but such messages takes time to permeate the minds of the at-risk as Mike found out.

Getting Mentee to Understand Proves Difficult:

> On my first day I was assigned to mentor Brad. After our introduction and talking to him for a while, I got the feeling that we bonded almost right away…
>
> The second time I visited Brad, he was sitting quietly at the opposite end of the classroom. I eased over next to him to find out what was going on, but all he said was, "He made me mad," and pointed to the classroom monitor… Eventually he and I had a chance to talk. I told him that he needed to control his anger and gave him some tips on how to go about it… When the time came to do his schoolwork, he pouted and whined about the things he didn't want to work on. At one point he got up and went to the time-out room on his own. I followed him and coerced him to go back to the classroom and do his reading assignment… I

> explained to him the importance of learning to read, and why reading is more important for black people, especially when we have been denied these same books for so long. I told him that many of the people who fought for the right to an education were his grandmothers and grandfathers, who can't continue anymore. After explaining the importance of reading and what it did for me, I told him I was leaving. He quietly said, "I don't want you to leave, I want you to help me." From that moment, I knew something had gotten over him. Either my words convinced his soul a little, or it is the sincerity in which it was done. Whatever the reason, he took it to heart...
>
> Considering the fun Brad and I had last weekend, I visited him on Thursday with renewed confidence... We practiced his reading skills with a timer, and he handled all the sections real well finishing before the time was up. He even wanted to read more than what the teacher required... Brad is doing well, and it seems I am getting through to him. I am hoping that we will be able to spend more good times together...
>
> Last Thursday was hell. It almost made me regret everything I was trying to do for Brad... It seemed I was doing everything in my power to get across to him, but it looks like every time something positive happens, Brad throws something negative back. I got frustrated which was unusual... It angers me to know that I spend so much time directing him one way and he does the opposite. It's like we worked so hard on building a trusting relationship, at least that's what I thought, and in the end we hadn't made any progress at all, (Mentor: Michael).

Michael continued to work with Brad without much success. When Michael graduated, Brad was reassigned another mentor.

THINGS TO REMEMBER

- Mentors must not mistakenly assume that because they come from similar backgrounds and share common ethnicity as their mentees they will be successful in their mentoring efforts.
- While the lived experiences of hardship, poverty and success can be shared, these cannot be readily transferred from mentor to mentee.
- The lessons of poverty are varied and often difficult to translate in meaningful ways.
- Poverty affects the lives, personalities and temperaments of at-risk youths in dissimilar ways. Even at-risk youths from the same households are likely to be affected by poverty differently.

DISCUSSION QUESTIONS AND EXERCISES

1. Do you believe that a mentor's lived experiences of poverty can be transferred to the mentee? Explain.

2. Outline your views on poverty and compare these with the lived realities of your mentee.

3. Do you consider similar family background and common ethnicity to be prerequisites in selecting a mentee? Explain

4. What could Michael have done to improve his relationship with Brad?

CHAPTER 13

To Effectively Provide Guidance and Assistance to At-Risk Youths, Mentors Must be Continuously Trained.

Necessity for Training:

Crucial to the success of a mentoring program is the training mentors receive. Training must take place continuously, and incorporate both the theoretical and practical aspects of mentoring. It should not be assumed that because someone is an adult or a parent that he or she possesses the requisite skills and knowledge to be a successful mentor. While adulthood and parenthood may be important criteria in the selection of a mentor, neither of these characteristics should be deemed as the primary determinant for successful mentoring. Although adults and parents may have regular contacts with a large number of children, they may yet be distant from, ill equipped or unprepared to deal with the problems and vicissitudes of at-risk children. As one student-mentor puts it, "I felt that as a mother who has successfully raised three adult children, I was prepared to help a young child, but I was wrong. I never imagined that an eight year old could have so many personal problems from understanding simple instructions and being inattentive, to displaying anger and refusing to respond to everything," (Mentor: Regina).

Expressions of unpreparedness are to be expected in the early stages of the mentoring process. However, with training, mentors are likely to gain greater self-confidence as they acquire hands-on experience with their mentees while continuing to be trained.

Training Helps to Understand Poverty:

For many mentors, the consequences of poverty on the lives of at-risk youths can bring about a sort of culture shock. Especially in situations where mentors lack adequate training, many can easily become overwhelmed when coming face to face with the dire consequences of poverty, especially on the lives of severely at-risk youths. However, with adequate preparation and training on the complexities of at-riskness, mentors would be better prepared for the task of mentoring the at-risk including, the severely at-risk as observed in the following account.

A Mentee's Will to Survive

> The more I tried to understand the life of Willie, the more complex it presents itself. The problems that the teacher and I faced on a daily basis with Willie is not what caught my attention on this day; it is the way he is dressed, with a wrinkled white shirt, faded green pants and black shoes with no socks. The first thing that entered my mind is, how in the world can someone send their child that they love, to school in this manner. Another thing I noticed about Willie is that he scratched his thighs in a vigorous manner. After noticing this behavior for a few minutes, I asked him if he had taken a bath before coming to school. Willie responded, "Why did you ask me that question?" I paused for a while and then asked another question. "Where are your socks?" he responded by saying that he had forgotten to put them on…
>
> When it was time for me to leave, I went up and hugged Willie and told him I love him. On my way out, the teacher stopped me and told me she has something to tell me. Nothing prepared me for what she said to me. The teacher told me that Willie was not living with his mother but with his uncle. While living there, his uncle and a friend got into an argument after drinking and the uncle was killed. Willie was at home at the time of the shooting. To add salt to Willie's injury, his mother was incarcerated for drug possession. After the death of his uncle, Willie used his bicycle to move around, going from aunt to aunt, but would go back to his uncle's place to get prepared for school. When the school found out, Social Services were called to take care of the situation. Then, one of his aunts stepped forward to take custody of him…
>
> After learning of all of Willie's problems, I became sad, but was happy that he was still in school and I am his mentor. I have become even more supportive of Willie, a sort of big brother. I try to apply some of the things I learned in class, things such as, if you let your mentees see that you genuinely care for them, they will reciprocate. I continue to encourage Willie and keep on telling him that he can be anything he wants to be. Now, every time before I leave him I give him a hug and tell him, "I love you

> Willie." Yesterday when I did this Willie gave me a huge hug and said, "I love you too Len," (Mentor: Len).

Currently, Willie has another mentor since Len left to take up an internship with a government agency.

An aspect of mentoring that can become quite frustrating for mentors is teaching academic subjects to at-risk youths, with learning deficiencies. *On the one hand, at-risk youths with learning problems usually have difficulties understanding simple instructions, paying attention, and retaining information. On the other hand, adults serving as mentors seldom possess the necessary instructional skills, or receive training in teaching.* And, since most mentors serve as tutors, the mentor-tutor process could be quite intimidating for both mentors and mentees. While there is an abundance of instructional methods, there is no simple way to train mentors to teach educationally at-risk youths. Sometimes, the best way to prepare mentors to become tutors is through the use of examples. In the following conversation with Sammie, I learned that patience sometimes make better mentor-tutors. The following essay is regularly used to sensitize mentor-tutors to the educational struggles of at-risk youths, with learning problems.

We Can All Learn From Those With Learning Disabilities If Only We Try:

> Sammie stood by my office door for about thirty seconds, undecided whether to knock or just walk in. Conscious of her indecision, I invited her to come in and have a seat.
>
> "Do you need to talk to me about something?" I asked.
>
> "I want to talk to you about my mentee," she said softly. "He is a good little boy who needs a lot of help, but he is not getting the attention he needs."
>
> Having said this, Sammie shifted her gaze downwards and began toying with the pencil-holder on my desk. A few seconds elapsed before she raised her head to speak. I could see clearly the tears brimming in her eyes. Impulsively, I wanted to get up and console her, to reassure her that everything would be alright, but for some unknown reason I seemed unable to reach out to her. She had not said much. Was the problem her mentee, or was it personal? Was the class assignment too difficult? Was she apprehensive about the up coming exam? These questions raced quickly through my mind. Then, as gently as possible, I coaxed Sammie into telling

me why she thought her mentee needed help and why he was not getting it.

"I was diagnosed with a learning disability as a child, and I could see the symptoms in Ben," she said almost in a whisper… "My teachers were not trained to deal with my problem. My classmates mocked me. Everyone seemed to think I was dumb, that I couldn't learn anything, that I was abnormal… I know, I was there, I understand, yet I am helpless. It pains my heart."

As Sammie talked about her learning problems of childhood, I could sense that she felt an affinity with Ben. She assured me repeatedly that she understood his problems, his discomforts, his pain, and most of all his silence. In Ben she saw a truly misunderstood child. In Ben, she saw someone not with a learning disability, but a child who needed specialized instruction. In Ben, she saw a child who was left to suffer the consequences of exclusion. In Ben, she saw not only the stress and frustration of coping with school, but also a reflection of herself. She felt his loneliness. She shared his exclusion, his pain, and his moments of quiet isolation. "Ben is not a bad kid. He is not dumb. I know I can help him if only I can make his teacher understand him," Sammie said.

Recognizing Sammie's commitment to help Ben, I inquired further into her own learning problems and how she dealt with them. She explained that as early as elementary school, she found education to be quite intimidating. Classroom instructions were not individualized and made little sense. Simple things appeared quite complex. Often this led to frustration that further inhibited learning. As soon as she learned the classroom material, she would forget; this led to being ignored by some of her teachers. "It is not their fault she said apologetically. "They had so many other students to deal with, I was only one." However, she continued to explain that because schools emphasize pass rates on standardized tests, she was never rewarded for her efforts, and she felt rebuffed for not scoring well on these tests.

I asked Sammie how she was able to overcome some of her learning problems. "Oh! My mother is a schoolteacher and she worked long hours with me," she replied.
"Was learning very painful?"
"Yes, especially because I forgot things easily… Once, my mom was trying so hard to make me understand simple math, I became

> confused. The harder she tried, the less I understood. My mom knew how hard I was trying, but I couldn't grasp it. I then began to cry uncontrollably. Knowing how I felt brought tears to my mom's eyes… As we hugged each other and cried, my mom kept saying, don't worry Baby, I will see you through this even if it kills me… This only made me cry harder. But thanks to my mom, I am in college today."
>
> At various points in our conversation, I found myself attempting to peer into Sammie's thoughts in an effort to fuse with her feelings. Each time I tried, I failed. As if she sensed my efforts, Sammie said: "my teachers never understood my struggles to cope. They did not understand my emotional pain. How could they? They did not have my disability." The directness of the last sentence seemed to have awakened me from my efforts to grasp her feelings. Yet, I kept reminding myself of how little I understood of Sammie's world, the shame, the guilt, the fear, the ostracism. "How was she able to cope?" I asked myself. In my quiet contemplation, I began to wonder about the Bens out there in our schools who are unable to share their feelings about their learning disabilities. Do they, like Sammie, receive assistance that would enable them to become successful students?
>
> For over two months, Sammie made every effort to assist Ben with his schooling, and from all reports she was succeeding. Then, one day, almost breathless, she returned to my office with the same sad expression on her face as before. "Ben's family moved and I don't know where they went," she said haltingly. I immediately assured her that she had done her best, and that I am convinced that Ben benefited from her tutelage. "You are a remarkable person Sammie," I said with conviction. "I hope I can become as sensitive as you are to those who have learning problems. I am not too old to learn, am I?" My comments must have struck a chord with Sammie. She looked straight at me, and with a gentle smile, she replied: "You sure can learn from Dr. Persaud, if only you try." You are right Sammie, I quietly concluded. We can all learn from those with learning disabilities, if only we try.

The example of Sammie helps to sensitize us to some of the difficulties in mentoring someone with learning disabilities. Since more and more at-risk youths are classified with learning disabilities, mentors are likely to find the mentoring activity increasingly challenging.

Anger Management:

In mentoring at-risk youths, many mentors will find themselves placed in situations, or circumstances where they will have to assist their mentees in managing their anger or mediating their conflicts. As noted before, the large proportion of at-risk youth grow up under harsh conditions of deprivation, which often result in various forms of physical and emotional abuse. The deprivation, as well as the abuses, has caused many of these youths to develop anger, which often leads to aggression and sometimes violence. Already vulnerable, at-risk youths are driven deeper into anger and frustration when they find themselves negatively labeled with ADHD and other learning disabilities. Sometimes, for some unknown reason the anger and frustration could result in open aggression. Gloria's mentee serves as an example.

A Mentee's Aggression

> This week was quite a disappointing one. David's teacher pointed out that he was giving her "an attitude' all morning. I tried to get him to talk to me, but I was not having any luck. I tried to get him out of the classroom, to go to the library and check out a book, but I was not successful. I then asked him if he wanted to go outside with the other students. He agreed. As we made our way out of the classroom, David got into a fight with one of his classmates. They had gone to get a football, so that they could play flag football, when one of the kids said something that ticked David off. He tried to fight back, but the other student Ken punched him in the face. David then grabbed Ken. I grabbed David and another teacher who was present grabbed Ken and the two were separated. David was absolutely infuriated. He was so angry that he was literally shaking and his eyes welled up with tears. As I was holding him back, he kept threatening me saying, "If you don't let go, I am going to hit you." I just kept telling him to calm down. There was nothing else I could do.
>
> David's teacher then came out and got David and Ken into the classroom where she placed them on "time-outs." Placed in a corner, David started to scream. Finally, when he calmed down, I was able to talk to him. I told him that he needed to calm down and not fight back, but he kept on threatening Ken. I told him that

> Ken was wrong, but that he didn't need to fight back. He seemed not to care. Before I left, I told him to promise me not to fight again but he just nodded his head.
>
> When I left David I felt horrible for him. I felt like I couldn't help him at all. The special class he is in is supposedly for children with behavioral problems. And, I can see now that David definitely has an anger problem, but I also realize that this class is not helping him. No one is telling him how to cope with his learning difficulties and how to react without anger, (Mentor: Glory).

To be able to assist such youths as David and Ken, mentors must be given adequate training in anger management and conflict mediation. In this regard, mentors must be trained to play several roles which includes being a: (a) **mediator**:- coaching mentees how to deal with the conflict constructively; (b) **penalizer**:- imposing sanctions on the mentees' misconduct; and (c) **healer**:- helping mentees work through the underlying aggression and anger (see Barsky, 2000).

THINGS TO REMEMBER

- The training of mentors is crucial to the mentoring process. People should not assume that because they are parents, or literate adults that these experiences readily qualify them to become successful mentors.
- Without training, mentors are likely to suffer the *culture shock of poverty* in this society of abundance.
- Training alerts mentors to the complexities of poverty and the varied consequences on the lives of at-risk youths.
- Through training and regular workshops, mentors would be able to acquire skills in patterns of communication, anger management, conflict mediation, antisocial personality disorder, and working with individuals with learning disabilities etc.

DISCUSSION QUESTIONS AND EXERCISES

1. Why is training important in mentoring an at-risk youth?

2. Assuming that you were assigned to mentor Willie, prepare an assessment of him and explain the steps you would take in assisting him.

3. Explain the approach you would take in mentoring an at-risk youth who has learning difficulties.

4. Can we learn from those with learning disabilities? Explain.

5. What are the lessons to be learned from Sammie's experience of mentoring Ben?

6. How would you go about assisting your mentee to manage his/her anger?

CHAPTER 14

Given the Level of Mistrust Common Among At-risk Youths, Mentor-Mentee Reciprocal Trust Must Constantly be Pursued

Trust vs. Mistrust:

Eric Erickson in his book *Childhood and Society* (1950) noted that trust is crucial in the development of children. Trust, he noted, starts from infancy, and sets the stage for the individual life long expectations of trustworthiness from himself and from others. Children who receive good care, emotional warmth, comfort and security will develop a sense of competence and trustfulness of others, while those who are denied such care and attention will become mistrustful of others and their surroundings. Among at-risk youths, many have become mistrustful of adults, as a result of the inconsistent treatment they received from their parents and significant others in their lives. **Given such predisposition to mistrust among at-risk youths, mentor-mentee reciprocal trust must, therefore, be constantly pursued and reinforced.** In the initial stages of mentoring, mentors may assume that since they are voluntarily providing much needed services, they would or should be trusted. Upon discovering that they are not trusted, mentors could become perplexed, confused or may even be dismayed. Such feelings of rejection could easily lead to contemplation of withdrawal from serving as a mentor as evident from Lisa's experience.

A Mentee's Mistrust Leads to Rejection

When I went to the school, I was assigned Shanika. She is a fourth grader. At first glance she seemed like a pleasant child, but as I started to work with her, I discovered that she was not paying attention, nor seem to care about learning. She would not stay focused and frequently got up to perform unrelated activities…

It is now my fifth visit and I don't know what I am doing wrong. I am ready to give up. Maybe mentoring is not for me. Shanika still does not pay much attention. I know she is classified as having a learning disability, but I am still puzzled that she hardly

> pays attention to schoolwork or to me. In my desperation, I promised her I would take her a small present on my next visit. I hope something good comes out of it…
> Today, as soon as I arrived at the school Shanika was waiting for me. Before I could say anything Shanika asked, "Did you bring my present? Did you bring my present?" When I told her that I did, she wanted to have it right away. When I refused to give her the present, she became angry and ran off… After some urging, I was able to get Shanika to go to the library with me. She did so only after I showed her the present, a little make-up kit with powder, a comb, bows and a small mirror…
> I spent over an hour and forty-five minutes with Shanika, talking to her and playing with her. I discovered that she has a hard time trusting anyone, and that she moved around a lot, living with her aunt, her grandmother and mother. When her mother takes her to her aunt or grandmother's house, she would promise to come back for her, but it always took a few days before she returned. Shanika thinks her mother loves her little brother more than her because her mother always takes him wherever she goes and never leaves him anywhere… When I asked her if she trusted me she responded, "ah ah", and when I asked why, she said, "cause you would leave me and don't come back." I assured her that I will see her again and that if I should leave I will get her "a nicer mentor." She laughed when I said that, (Mentor: Lisa).

In her later visits, Lisa continued to make clear that she had to work constantly to secure Shanika's trust and that she felt she was always being scrutinized by this little girl. Lisa's experience of mistrust from her mentee is not uncommon. Among at-risk youths, the denial of parental or adult care, affection and attention is quite common. Too often, their fathers and other adults move in and out of at-risk youths' lives, each time leaving them with a greater degree of mistrust. As the level of mistrust increases, many at-risk youths soon withdraw into their own worlds of security. Such experience of mistrust and withdrawal is vividly captured by Jonetta Barras in her book *Whatever Happened to Daddy's Little Girl.*

Barras wrote that by the time she became eight she had had three fathers. She explained the emptiness and unworthiness she felt as each of her fathers came in and out of her life. She vividly captured how each departure left a bigger and bigger void, which she struggled to fill by withdrawing into the quietness of her room. Barras then went on to describe in some detail how the mistrust carried over into her adult life and how it affected her relationship with men. She wrote (Barras, 2000:115-116):

> The triple fears—rejection, abandonment, and commitment—often boil down to the basic issue of trust. As much as I loved Willie, I couldn't trust him to return the next day. I couldn't trust that what we shared was enough, that he could really make a commitment to me and mean it.
>
> After all, my fathers had made a commitment, hadn't they? Didn't Bill promise to love my mother forever? Didn't Noel say he loved me? Hadn't he just walked away, never to be seen or heard from again? … The fatherless daughter is afraid to trust any man, believing him capable of doing the same thing as her father—abandoning her, rejecting her.

The life of mistrust described by Barras is experienced daily by many at-risk African American youths. Among at-risk youths, mistrust appears to be quite pervasive thereby requiring the constant pursuit of mentor-mentee reciprocal trust. For many, growing up under abysmal conditions of poverty, where fathers are absent, and where familial discord and abuse are commonplace, mistrust has become a way of life. As one seven year old in the course of a conversation once said to me, "My gramma says done trust nobady." When I asked her why, she said, "Ah dunno, cause what my gramma says." Such expressions of mistrust are not unusual, especially in the early stages of mentoring. During this period, mentees are most likely to be cautious given their lived experiences. Mentors must therefore be alert when seeking to establish trust. They must be mindful of their own actions and words of promise, and make every effort not to underestimate the sensitivities of their young mentees. Stephen became aware of what a promise means to his mentee during his second week of mentoring. He wrote:

> I arrived at the center at my usual time of 4:00 p.m., and when I walked in Bri was excited to see me. He said: "You did not lie to me, you really did come back." I then began to reflect on some material that was covered in my mentoring class, and started to wonder if the child has had a lot of promises broken so early in his young life. He seemed so happy by the simple fact that I kept my promise and came back to see him. I wonder what goes on in his little mind when people don't keep the promises they made to him.

I wonder what he would have done if I had not kept my promise to him… (Mentor: Stephen).

Sometimes the degree of mistrust is so deep-seated, mentors have to work harder to establish trust. Since reasons for the mistrust are hidden within the minds of the mentees, mentors must be forced to strive harder to win trust. This, however, is easier said than done especially since it is extremely difficult to break into the inner thoughts and feelings of children who hardly say much. In the following, Derek explained how by coincidence he was able to break into mentee Darrell's feelings, and winning his trust.

Finding the Source of Mistrust Accidentally:

It is now three weeks and Darrell is still not saying anything much. He still refuses to read or do anything I ask. Whenever I put a book in front of him, he would just gaze quietly at it. Sometimes I find myself talking non-stop for fifteen minutes straight. I have never seen a child who refuses to respond to everything I tried… I had a lengthy conversation with his teacher and she explained that Darrell tries to complete his assignments, but would not say much of anything…

After I opened up Darrell's case to our class discussion last week, I decided to visit Darrell's neighborhood. When I arrived, I saw Darrell playing in the parking lot with some of his friends. I also noticed Chris from Darrell's class. As soon as I got out of my car Chris greeted me, and asked if I was there to see Darrell. I answered "yes." Unlike Chris, Darrell did not come up to greet me right away, so I went to my car, took the basketball I carried around in it and threw it to Darrell. I told him he and his friends could play with it. Since there was no hoop, I told them we could go to the schoolyard and play. As soon as Darrell heard this he threw the ball back to me and ran home…

On my next visit to school, I explained to Darrell's teacher what happened over the weekend when I visited Darrell's neighborhood. She explained that Darrell and two of his friends were picked up by the police during one summer for trespassing on school property. As soon as she told me, I felt that this was Darrell's problem with school. I then made up a story of how, when I was a kid, I was charged with trespassing on school property and that it made me hate school, and how I don't trust the police. Darrell listened carefully but didn't say much. When I was ready to leave, Darrell asked me if I cried when I was picked

up by the police. I then made up the story of how much I cried and how scared I was. Darrell then told me how he and his friends were picked up for playing in the schoolyard and going into the school because they knew the door was open…
We went out to sit at a table in the schoolyard and I asked Darrell to describe his arrest. I let him tell me about it at least twice. I then slapped him five and told him we are now buddies since we were both arrested for trespassing on school property. He laughed so much I thought he was a different person… Darrell is now responding to me much better.

The lack of trust, due to the denial of parental care and attention, or the arrest experience suffered by Darrell is a common occurrence among at-risk African American youths. And, on occasions when the mistrust is accompanied by emotional, physical or sexual abuse, the disconnected youths customarily seek refuge in a life of sexual promiscuity, crime and drugs. To have some understanding of how deep seated mistrust and emotional abuse can lead to sexual promiscuity, we turn to Barras. She (2000:89) stated:

> I go from house to house, from bed to bed, from wrong man to wrong man—sometimes a right man but for the wrong reason. I proclaim victory where there has been none. And I declare defeat far too prematurely; it is a case of the "un"s—"unwanted and unlovable." Thus unlove song is backed up by the constant chorus of triple fears. The wisdom is, of course, sculpted from hindsight.

Barras' words to some extent find expression in the notations of one mentor.

Mistrust Sometimes Leaves Mentee Vulnerable to Exploitation

> Carla was fourteen years old when I first met her. Her grandmother had called the Role Model Program seeking help for her. From Carla's grandmother I learned that Carla was under her care and that she was worried, because Carla would leave home in the evenings and does not return until the next day. I also learned that Carla's mother was a drug addict, who had no time for Carla or her brother.

My first meeting with Carla was at her middle school. Danielle, Tanika and I went to Carla's school because we all felt sorry for her grandmother and wanted to help. At school, we found Carla playing with four boys in the schoolyard. They all seemed to be having a good time. After we introduced ourselves, we asked Carla to join us under a tree. From the very beginning Carla was anxious to talk about herself. She told us she was very popular at school and that she preferred the company of boys than girls. As I mentored Carla over the next few months, I began to learn a lot more about her life. On the outside she seemed like a happy girl, but inside she carried a lot of pain. She felt she could not trust the adults around her…

According to Carla, she is not sure who her father is although she heard he was her mother's cousin. She said that as far as she can remember, she knew her mother had a lot of boy friends. When she was eight she was molested by her uncle who was always drunk or on drugs. She did not know she was being molested at the time. When she was thirteen she said her uncle raped her and when she tried to tell her mother she became angry and beat her for telling lies. The rape continued, then one day she had the courage to tell her grandmother and she took her in to live with her. She believes that her grandmother is her savior, the only person who loves her.

At school, Carla is not doing very well and constantly fights with other girls. She told me that she once beat another girl for "going with her boy friend." When I asked about the boy friend, she said he was twenty-four years old and has a nice car, and that he cares for her. She said he always gives her money and buys her presents. She then showed me a watch he bought for her. I asked her if she stays out at nights with her boyfriend. She said he has a nice apartment and sometimes she goes to sleep over there…

Over the six months, I worked with Carla she never expressed much interest in school. Most of the time, she wanted to talk about her boy friend. Once when I asked if she was using drugs she answered, "Only when I am with my boy friend." She said she would do anything for her boyfriend because he loves her. When I told her she was too young to have an affair with an older man, she sucked her teeth…

Three weeks ago Carla told me she thought she was pregnant. Yesterday she called to say she was not. When Carla called, I told her it was close to exam time and that I would see her in two weeks. Yesterday, I went to her grandmother's house, but no one was at home. When I called her grandmother today, she said Carla was arrested for drug possession. I never heard from her nor saw her again (Mentor: Toya).

Subsequent attempts to locate Carla proved unsuccessful. Several months passed when we received information that she was in a correctional facility.

THINGS TO REMEMBER

- It is incorrect for mentors to assume that because they provide services voluntarily that they would be readily accepted and trusted by their mentees.
- Many at-risk youths have become mistrustful of adults because of inconsistent parental care and affection, or mistreatment they have received from significant adults in their lives.
- Depending on the mentees' levels of mistrust, mentors are likely to be faced with varying degrees of rejection and indifference. Such adverse behaviors must be dealt with in order to effectively provide mentoring services.
- No two at-risk mentees, even from the same household, experience mistrust in the same exact way. Hence, a canned approach to identifying and addressing mistrust is likely to be unsuccessful.

DISCUSSION QUESTIONS AND EXERCISES

1. What are some of the reasons why many at-risk youths distrust adults?

2. What would do if you found out that your mentee suffers from mistrust?

3. Shanika appears to have difficulty trusting anyone: Why? What would you have done to win her trust?

4. Explain how Derek was able to win the trust of Darrell. Would you have done the same? Explain.

5. Discuss how Carla's mistrust left her vulnerable to exploitation?

6. What would you have done to win Carla's trust and assist her with her problems?

CHAPTER 15

Cultural Sensitivity and Adaptability are Two Prerequisites for Successful Mentoring

Cultural Literacy:

Among the key factors to the successful mentoring of at-risk African American youths is an understanding and sensitivity of their cultural complexities and how these influence and shape their lives. The acquisition of such an understanding is referred to as **cultural literacy**. "Cultural literacy helps to form the basis for inclusion by highlighting both past and potential contributions by diverse peoples. It argues for retaining rather than relinquishing cultural identity as a means for them to move into and be an integral part of the larger society," (Ogawa 1999:18). Applied to mentoring, the acquisition of cultural literacy would enable mentors to understand how African American culture fashions the worldview, the mode of existence and uniqueness of the at-risk African American youth population. It would help sensitize mentors to such cultural complexities as race and class, and how these contribute to African American youths' perceptions and definitions of Self and their constructions of social reality. Moreover, cultural literacy world enable mentors to acquire **cultural competence**. As defined by Lum (1999:29), cultural competence is "the ability to understand the dimensions of culture and cultural practice and apply them to the client and the cultural/social environment." It includes "knowledge and interpersonal skills to understand, appreciate, and work with individuals and families from cultures other than one's own," (Lum 2003:12). Lacking in cultural literacy and competency, mentors are likely to be insensitive to the realities of African Americans at-risk youths and approach mentoring with negative stereotypic views of this group. Such stereotypic views include the belief that these youths come from "dysfunctional' families, have learning deficiencies (therefore, constitute the vast majority of special education students), are aggressive, and therefore, have propensities toward delinquent behaviors.

I Once Believed Dysfunctional Families Existed.

> Although I am an African American, I was not sensitized to the problems of my people. I attended predominantly White schools and had little interaction with African Americans from all socio-economic levels. With both of my parents being professionals, we lived in a predominantly White middle class neighborhood, where most of our friends were Whites and middle class African Americans. Since we lived in Illinois, several States away from my parents' families, we never had much contact with all our cousins and relatives...
>
> On my first day of mentoring, I was shocked. When I entered the classroom, all I saw was a bunch of noisy children, some of whom were walking around the classroom picking on others. I wanted to quit being a mentor, but then I remembered some of the statements from the first lecture. "Mentoring is not for everyone. If you can't develop an understanding and appreciation for disadvantaged youths, then don't become a mentor... If you have a heart, a willingness to learn and would like to help a poor child, then stick it out... Being poor does not make a child a criminal."..
>
> I must admit that when I started out mentoring, I felt that children are aggressive and delinquent because they come from single parent dysfunctional families. As I worked with Ebony and got to know her and her mother, I realized how wrong I was about single parents and their poor children. Ebony's mother worked two jobs so that she could provide for her children. She hopes one day to have a home of her own. How can she be called dysfunctional? If she is, then I too am dysfunctional and so too are those who stereotype her, (Mentor: Pamela).

Through her mentoring activities, Pamela was able to reassess her perspective on dysfunctional families and question the validity of such a label. It is not unusual for adults to undertake the mentoring of an at-risk child with cultural biases of disadvantaged families' structure and relations. Such preconceived notions usually give rise to misunderstandings which frustrate and negatively impact the mentoring relationship. It is essential for adults to approach mentoring with a great degree of cultural neutrality if they are to succeed.

Cultural Diversity:

Although we live in a multicultural society, many of us are insensitive to, or intolerant of the diversity of cultures that surround us, including that of Africans. The general tendency is to expect every racial and ethnic group to assimilate to the dominant culture. For some ethnic groups, assimilation is relatively easy; for others, the process becomes difficult because of various barriers erected through social policies, oppression, unequal opportunities or racism etc. that they must overcome. Among the diverse groups in America today, African Americans undoubtedly have had enormous difficulties in assimilating to the dominant culture. While several obstacles hinder African American assimilation, the most pronounced include social and economic inequality and racism. As noted earlier in this monograph, African Americans, in order to succeed, must adapt to two different social cultural worlds, their own and that of the dominant group. But, in the process of assimilating to the world of the dominant group they often experience resistance because of their race, and the many forms of institutional racism, which marginalizes them (Feagin 1999; Knowles and Prewitt 2001).

African Americans, more so than any other groups, are regularly compared with more recent immigrant arrivals to show their lack of success in a land of endless opportunities. **However, what most of these comparisons fail to emphasize, is that the new immigrants did not suffer with the same degree of intensity, the indignities of slavery, discrimination, oppression, racism, segregation, denial of educational and economic opportunities, dehumanization, and more recently, racial profiling and higher rates of incarceration, as African Americans.** These indignities stripped almost completely, African Americans of their cultural uniqueness. While African Americans had to reconstruct their cultural traditions from the residues of an oppressive historical past, the newly arrived immigrants simply brought with them their cultures and transplanted them wherever they settled.

Like all other ethnic groups in our society, the everyday realities of African American youths are grounded within their social-cultural context. It is therefore essential for mentors to adopt a "cultural neutrality" approach, which seeks to integrate assistance within the cultural framework of the mentees, rather than work in opposition to it. **Any mentoring assistance, no matter how well intentioned, is likely to be counter productive if it seeks to impose on the youthful African mentees social-cultural values and beliefs that are inconsistent with their culture.** Too often, knowingly or unknowingly, mentors adopt the ethnocentric approach, which cause them to make judgments from the perspective of their own culture. Whenever such cultural imposition occurs, it usually causes frustration and impedes the mentoring process. This is made clear in the case of William and his mentee Alex.

When William decided to become a mentor, he was assigned to work with Alex a fourteen-year-old at-risk African American. Alex's grandmother had specifically requested that we assign him to someone who can help him academically, as well as guide him in the right direction by "getting his mind off the street." Believing that he could help Alex turn his life around, William opted to mentor him. Almost from the start, the relationship between William and Alex became confrontational.

Culture Clash:

> William, who left the Caribbean with his parents to reside in United States, takes pride in his Caribbean heritage, values education, and spent much of his time reading and preparing for college. Although he lived a few years in Miami, he and his sister did not associate much with African Americans. Because of the large concentration of immigrants in the area where their parents resided, they were able to establish relationships with youths from various Caribbean islands. According to William, he and his friends anxiously looked forward to the day they would be going to college. They competed academically, and as he puts it, "had an easy time in high school."
>
> Being proud of his Caribbean upbringing and his high regard for education, William became offended when Alex refused to read the works of Caribbean writers he had given him. William explained that he enjoyed the books he gave to Alex. "These books opened up a whole new world for me when I was small, and they would too for him if he reads them," William insisted. He

> continued: "One of Alex's main problems is that he listens to too much rap music which teaches too much violence, not how to think. We listened to Reggae and Calypso which always have messages in them." When asked if he tried to introduce Alex to Reggae and Calypso he said, "Yes," but that Alex laughed at him. As he explained, "One day as I was giving Alex a ride home from school, I played Bob Marley for him. He asked me what craziness is that. When I explained the meaning, he laughed and repeated 'come down man, come down man' and laughed again. William concluded by saying that, "Alex does not know what's good for him and that he would not get very far with such an attitude."

In the process of mentoring, the mentors should always be alert to their own ethnocentric ideals. Ethnocentrism clouds one's objectivity and serves as a barrier to accepting that there *is* another way, another belief, another communication style, another custom, or another value that can lead to culturally different behavior." Shusta et., al. (1995:19). The case of William and Alex helps to demonstrate that a mentor could easily try to impose his cultural values and beliefs on a mentee.

Class Differences:

While cross-cultural differences can affect the mentoring relationship, within-cultural differences can also produce frustrations for the mentor and mentee. *Electing to become mentors to at-risk African American youths, many African American adults regularly come face to face with the cultural variants within their own culture.* Raised primarily in middle class, upper-middle class families, these individuals have achieved or experienced some level of economic success and want to "give back" to their communities. Residing in Black middle class communities or integrated neighborhoods, they have accommodated to the normative patterns and lifestyles of their communities, which sometimes clash with the cultural realities of disadvantaged Americans. If not carefully dealt with, the cultural differences can become problematic for the mentoring relationship. The experience of Tanya will help to illustrate the conflict within culture and how she dealt with it.

Tanya, an African mother of three lived in a mixed middle class neighborhood. When she heard that Melvin, an eight-year-old

African American male needed assistance, she volunteered to be his mentor. She felt that since Melvin lived only a mile from her and was the same age as her son, she would be able to offer him the assistance he needed. During the first three months of mentoring, Tanya experienced some difficulties with Melvin's behavior which she had to address. In the following account, Tanya explains the difference in parenting styles between her and Melvin's mom and how she dealt with it.

Parenting While Mentoring:

> Melvin and his mother were dropped off at my home today... Melvin immediately went upstairs looking for my children and he looked around the house a little. He feels at home here and that is very important, because it tells me that he is comfortable here, and he knows that he is welcome to go to any part of the house that he would like to.
>
> They played outside for a little while, and then we went to the Science center. We started the day out late but Melvin was able to see and became very interested in all the things the Center has to offer. There was a safe room that was built for hurricanes and tornadoes. There was also a lot of artwork and exhibits. After a while, Melvin's behavior became a little rough. I think it may be because his mother came along. He wanted to show off. I could tell that he had never been there, just as he told me he has never been to Applebee's and a lot of other places.
>
> After leaving the museum, we went to the grocery store. After that we went to McDonalds. Melvin was doing things that a normal child would do, such as being loud, playing in the store etc. Every time his mother told him to be quiet or do something, he refused. His mother loves him, I can tell that. She gave him the last bit of money that she had, and she bought him a kid's meal. He asked me for one, and I told him that everyone was getting a sandwich or chicken nuggets, and that I was going to buy two large orders of fries for them to split. He was upset, so his mother told him she would buy him a kid's meal. I told her she should not have given in. I gave Melvin's mother an apple pie that was given to me for being patient. She gave it to Melvin who claimed it as his, and then he refused to share it with her when she asked him for a piece of it. He then gave her a tiny piece.

> We then left for the fun station. On our way Melvin's mother was scolding him about something, and he really "got smart" with her. I explained to him that while I was his mentor, I would not tolerate him being disrespectful to his mother, and if he was disrespectful to the woman who gave birth to him, what does he think about me? I told him that any other place we go, he will have to earn it, and that if he didn't apologize to his mother, I would take him home, and I meant it! I never make a promise and not follow through. Knowing that whenever I make a threat, I follow up on it, Melvin reluctantly apologized to his mother. I then explained to Melvin's mother why it was necessary for me to discipline him. As best as I could, I tried to let her understand that if Melvin continues to have his way, she may not be able to control his behavior. I told her she needs to put her foot down, and let him know who is queen, (Mentor: Tanya).

Tanya explained that she was not sure how Melvin's mother felt when she dropped them home that night. 'She hardly said much at the time." Two weeks later Melvin's mother called Tanya to thank her for mentoring Melvin, because she could see the positive changes in him.

Many middle class African American adults approach the task of mentoring with the conviction that they understand the plight of at-risk African American youths because they are of the same race. **While race may provide mentors easy access into the lives of their mentees, it does not automatically translate into having a better understanding of the problems of at-risk youths**. To the extent that many African Americans have become integrated into their middle class communities and neighborhoods, they have become equally distanced or even detached from the cultural realities of poor black neighborhoods. *In more ways than they realize, African American middle class mentors are just as isolated from the cultural realities of poverty as their at-risk African American mentees are distanced from the cultural realities of middle class existence.* It is therefore not uncommon for mentors to express their culture shock after a few weeks of mentoring. In the following example, Rodney expressed his disbelief regarding his mentee's family inability to pay fifty-five dollars in rent. Given their precarious economic circumstances and poor financial management skills, many disadvantaged families are forced to move for failure to pay their rent.

> "The first time Kenny told me they moved I didn't pay much attention. Then, three weeks ago when I asked him why he didn't do his homework, he said they moved to live with his aunt. Today, Kenny told me they moved again. I thought he was lying so I asked him how often they moved, he said "a lot." When I asked him what he meant by "a lot", he said eight or ten. When I asked him why they moved so much he said: "His momma can't pay the rent." I was shocked when he told me the rent was only fifty-five dollars a month. I kept thinking that my monthly rent is four hundred dollars and Kenny's mother can't even pay fifty-five dollars a month? (Mentor: Rodney).

The Mentee and Parentification:

While middle class African American mentors are aware of teenage parents, they are generally less aware of the culturally based custom of **parentification** among disadvantage African Americans. That is the situation in which, "One or both parents either consciously or unconsciously position(s) an underage child to assume roles or engage in child-rearing practices that are traditionally reserved for adults," (Anderson 1999:158). For most middle class African Americans whose views on parenting are shaped by their lived experiences or subscription to Euro-centric cultural values, the concept of parentification is not a part of their social cultural reality. In this next example, Latasha expressed her disbelief when she came face to face with the realities of family life of her ten year old mentee.

> Today, I visited Tanji's home for the second time. I was shocked to see her taking care of her five-year-old sister and two year old brother, while her mother was outside chatting with four men and one woman. Inside, Tanji's home was dark and hot. When I asked her why she does not turn on the lights, she said her mother told them not to so as to save on electricity. There was hardly any furniture in the house, except for the television and a broken sofa bed. As I watched Tanji feed her screaming brother and then change his clothes, my heart went out to her. How can a mother leave a little ten-year child to take care of two other children while she is outside having a good time with her friends? I know she is only twenty-five, but she is a mother. Why did she have so many children when she can't take care of them?...

> About an hour after, I left feeling very angry. I used to be angry at Tanji for not listening, for not doing her schoolwork. Now, I am angry at myself for not understanding her and her life, (Mentor: Latasha).

This is how Jodi-Ann captures the custom of parentification as it relates to at-risk youths:

> I sat back for a while today and just watched the children interact with each other. Many of them seemed so grown up already even though they are still in elementary school. I know a lot of them have been forced to become adults too fast. They sometimes complain to me that they have to watch their younger brothers and sisters when their mothers go out. These children seem like they need someone to take care of them. They are not old enough to take care of someone else. They are burdened with too much responsibilities.

In the forgoing illustrations of parentification, the reactions of mentees are that of surprise or disgust. For many at-risk youths, parentification is a fact of life, a part of their daily activities. Mentees burdened with parental responsibilities are likely to present greater challenges to the mentoring relationship. As mentor Jodi-Ann declared, "[These] children have a harder time in school and need more guidance… [they] always seem so irritated and do not want to pay attention. I wondered if the teachers at the Center have problems dealing with them… I always have to lighten up the situation by complementing them on their efforts"

Academically Unprepared Parents:

Quite often, mentors of all persuasion assume that parents can and should help their at-risk children academically. What this assumption does not take into consideration is the fact that many parents lack the time or academic preparation necessary to assist their children educationally. Many disadvantaged work extended hours to make ends meet, while others may not have finished high school. Furthermore, many disadvantaged parents today have no familiarity with computer-based instruction or the new methods of teaching and learning. As a result they are unable to assist their children who most often are at an educational disadvantage. Mentoring at a neighborhood center, one mentor observed that her mentee's mother neither assisted the mentee nor her brother or sister, all of whom attend the center. She noted that she had seen other mothers at the center working on the computers and other instructional aids with their children, but not the mother of her mentee. About her mentee's mother she wrote:

The mom is a story all by herself. She walks around the neighborhood with her hair bundled on top of her head, wears clothes that are too small and not fit for the season…I wonder what she sees when she looks at her children? Does she care that they are always dirty? It really upsets me how this mother does not seem to care for her children. Why is it that people who do not know these children, or have any connections to them, have to care about the children more than the mother does? She is never at the center to work with them like some of the other parents.

Verbal Interaction:

An aspect of mentoring which often highlights the cultural differences between mentors and mentees is that of verbal interaction. African American at-risk youth regularly adjust and readjust to the socio-linguistic expressions of their communities and the vernacular of their peer group. Since these expressions commonly deviate from formally accepted speech patterns and Standard English, mentors inclination would be to correct the linguistic expressions of their mentees. It is not uncommon for mentors to be convinced that their mentees' non-standard linguistic expressions transfer into the classroom setting and affect their academic progress. Correcting mentees use of non-standard English is therefore seen as a way to improve their academic performance.

> After Jeff completed his science assignment, I decided to talk to him so as to get to know him a little more. While he was telling me how strict his mother is, I happen to use the word "trippin." Jeff said, "It's about time you use a Black word." This really bothered me. "What do you mean talking White and talking Black, Jeff?" I asked. He responded, "White is how you talk." I then "tried" to educate Jeff on the use of proper English. However, I just received from him a very uninteresting stare.

> This experience tells me that children are taught the stereotypes of people in society. Therefore, they only know how to talk, act, and portray the typical stereotypic "Black person." If one does not try to correct this behavior in children, then as they grow older this behavior pattern will likely grow stronger, (Mentor: Widline).

On the surface, it may appear that mentors are making a positive contribution to their mentees education and academic progress by correcting their speech pattern. This view, however, is one-dimensional. It assumes that the linguistic expressions of African American at-risk youths are indicators of their academic performances. Mentors must therefore keep in mind that many people speak different dialects without being academically stereotyped in the same manner as at-risk African American youths. In addition, **mentors must take into consideration that Standard English is not the normative linguistic style within many ethnic communities, including the at-risk youths' communities**. Despite this deviation, the academic performances of people from these communities are not affected. Furthermore, by constantly correcting the idiomatic expressions of at risk youths may create frustration and serve to alienate them from the mentoring process. Mentors must therefore seek to understand the speech patterns of their mentees and ask questions that would facilitate reciprocal learning. This is what Brian did.

> Being White, I was not sure how Jamal would react to me. At first, he seemed withdrawn or cautious, but as the weeks passed he began to talk more and more. It took a while for me to understand everything he said. He would cut short some words like "because to "cause," speak incorrect English such as "Ah ain't tellin you noten," or use such terms as "chill" and "dog" frequently. In the beginning I just listened, but then, I started correcting him. As the weeks passed and I was correcting him more and more, Jamal became frustrated and gradually became less talkative. When I asked him what was wrong he said, "Cause you corecken evyting I says." I tried to explain that I was only trying to help him, but he refused to accept my explanation…
> Following up on our class discussion, instead of correcting Jamal, I decided to listen without correcting him. I also began asking him to explain terms that were not familiar to me. I remembered the first time I asked him to explain the word "crack head." He laughed for a few seconds and then pointing at me he said: "You

> don't know crack head?" and laughed again. He then took great pride in explaining to me that a crack head is a person who abuses crack cocaine… Now, when I talk to Jamal he would from time to time pause to explain some of the phrases without waiting for me to ask for explanations… In being more attentive to Jamal's assignments, I discovered that his written sentences were better than his spoken words, and that he was not as sensitive when I corrected his written work as when I corrected his speech, (Mentor: Brian).

Like Brian, many mentors often assume that their mentees would benefit if they correct the mentees' speech pattern. To what extent this assumption holds true is unclear. **Mentees are unlikely to adopt speech patterns that are incongruous with that of their neighborhood peers. Even if they adapt to a certain speech pattern while outside of their neighborhoods, they are likely to revert back to the acceptable patterns of their neighborhood peers.**

THINGS TO REMEMBER

- Cultural literacy and cultural competence are necessary prerequisites for the successful mentoring of at-risk youths.
- Cultural literacy and cultural competence necessitate the acquisition of knowledge and skills that would enable mentors to understand mentees, their families and their lived circumstances, and how these influence and impact their lives.
- The lack of cultural literacy/competence is likely to produce culture clash between mentors and mentees and result in poor mentoring outcomes.
- Cultural literacy and competency help foster effective interpersonal communication and interaction between mentors and mentees.

DISCUSSION QUESTIONS AND EXERCISES

1. Explain cultural literacy and discuss its' relevance to mentoring?

2. Drawing from Pamela's experience, would you say that she lacked the cultural competency necessary to assist her at-risk African American mentee? Explain.

3. Should African Americans be compared to recent immigrants in America?

4. How would you assess the culture clash between William and Alex? In your opinion, what should William have done to assist Alex?

5. Should class differences between mentor and mentee affect the mentoring relationship? Explain.

6. Tanya approached mentoring from the standpoint of a parent, what would you have done? Explain.

7. Supposing you found out that your young at-risk mentee shares some of the parenting responsibilities for his/her younger siblings, what would you do? Explain.

8. Explain how you would assist your mentee if you found out that his/her parent is inadequately prepared to provide him/her needed academic assistance.

9. Explain why verbal interaction is crucial to the mentoring process? Outline the steps you would take if your mentee's linguistic pattern differs from yours.

CHAPTER 16

Parents' Support and Participation in the Mentoring Effort Are Crucial for Success and Must Not be Underplayed.

The most widely practiced form of mentoring today is for mentors to provide tutoring services to mentees at locations away from their home environment. This is usually done without the involvement of the mentees parents in the mentoring process. It is true that most parents do grant permission for their at-risk children to have mentors. However, the mere granting of permission does not guarantee the success of the mentoring activity. *In order to achieve the maximum success possible, it is essential for mentors to have the support and participation of parents in the mentoring effort.*

Involving Mothers and Grandmothers:

For African American at-risk youths, many of whom are raised by their single-parent-mothers or grandmothers, it is crucial to involve these individuals directly and indirectly in the mentoring effort. Without the mothers or grandmothers involvement, the mentoring process is likely to have minimal effects on the mentees. At times, it may be necessary for a mentor to secure the support and participation of both mother and grandmother in the process. More often, such dual involvement becomes necessary in situations where the mother is either still young or receives assistance from the grandmother in raising the child. As already noted, it is a common practice among African American grandmothers, especially maternal grandmothers to be involved in the rearing of grandchildren. This involvement is even more intense among disadvantaged African American families, where grandmothers seek to alleviate some of the emotional and financial burdens of their youthful children who have become parents.

Some of the most frequently asked questions, or comments made regarding parental support in the mentoring process are: "Why do we need to involve parents when they can't help their children with their school work?" "Wouldn't parents slow the mentoring process down with all of their questions?" "How can parents contribute when many of them need help themselves?" Many parents have not completed high school themselves, what makes you think they would be interested in their children's education?" "Some parents don't seem to care about their children's education, why get them involved?" "What about parents who are addicted to drugs and alcohol, how do we involve them?"

It is quite easy for some mentors to question the necessity to involve parents in the mentoring process, especially if the parents are unable to assist or lack the necessary skills to provide the needed services to their mentored children. However, it should not be forgotten that parents and children are biologically and emotionally connected. Parents are therefore likely to disrupt the mentor-mentee relationship, whenever there is the perception that the mentoring efforts are excluding or marginalizing them from the lives of their children. Blechman (1992:166) explains the need for involving parents, especially single-mothers, in the mentoring process this way.

> Single mothers, ... may be more in need of mentoring than any of their children; without such help, single mothers may sabotage the mentor-protégé relationship... When the mentor ignores the needs of the single mother, the mentor risks either jeopardizing the mentor-protégé relationship or alienating the protégé from the family. However, when mentoring is extended to the single mother, the single mother may be better prepared to nurture the protégé and other siblings.

A mentor should not assume that because someone is a mother or father that he or she is a competent parent. Many young parents lack parenting skills, and are often not aware of or equipped to address the needs of their children. Under such circumstances, a mentor could provide much needed services to both parent and child.

Consequences of Excluding Parents:

Whenever parents feel excluded or marginalized, the common response is to withhold their children from participating in the mentoring process. Seldom is the withholding of children accompanied by any explanations. If mentors persist in their search for reasons, they are likely to receive polite explanations from parents who often seek to guise their feelings of threat.

> When Anika found out from a teacher that she would no longer be able to mentor Kim, a thirteen year old, she became confused. After repeated calls to Kim's house, she was unable to talk to Kim directly. Each time she called, Kim's mother would offer excuses ranging from "Kim is outside playing with her friends," to "Kim has gone out with her grandmomma and won't be back till late." As the excuses began to multiply, Anika became suspicious. She had visited Kim's home before and felt she had a fairly good relationship with mother and child. She therefore decided to go over to Kim's house, determined to get the real reason as to why she can no longer mentor Kim. As she explains:
>
> After receiving several excuses from Kim's mother as to why Kim was not returning my calls, I decided to pay her a visit. When I arrived, Kim was playing in the parking lot with some friends. As soon as she saw me, she ran up to me and whispered: "My Momma don't want you to be my mentor no more." When I asked why? She replied: "I don't know." I then went to see her mother. At first, Kim's mom seemed very uncomfortable, something I had never noticed before. After some small talk, I told her that if I offended her in any way, I was sorry. Picking up on what Kim had whispered to me, I told her that Kim is a smart child and that all I was trying to do was to help her, and that if I did anything wrong, I was truly sorry. At this point Kim's Mom interjected.
>
> "Ms. Anika, don't get me wrong, not dat I don't want Kim to see you no mo, but I can't do what you do for she, take her places, to the mall, get her hair done and such things. You know I can't afford these things with four children and all. Kim don't even want to help me much nomo. She prettied up sheself and watch sheself in the mirror, and all she says now is Ms. Anika says this, Ms. Anika says dat. Ms. Anika does her hair this way, everything is Ms. Anika. You know I care for my chilren, everyone of them."
>
> Realizing that Kim was emulating me instead of her mom, which to me seems to be the source of the problem, I got up from my chair and hugged her, reassuring her that Kim loves her very much, more than anyone else, including me. Since Kim always

> talks about her when she is with me, I informed her of this. I also reassured her that I would not do anything to hurt her or Kim, and that since she is only twenty eight and I am twenty two, I felt as if we were friends. I then said goodbye and walked out the door. As I was about to enter my car, Kim's Mom ran up behind me and said, "Ms. Anika, you can come pick up Kim tomora." I told her I would. (Anika continued to mentor Kim for another six months. She graduated and left for her hometown).

Parental disruption of the mentoring activity can even occur in situations where mentees suffer from neglect. Mentors should not assume that parents would welcome them to assist with their neglected children as Larry found out in mentoring nine-year-old Jason. Larry first met Jason when he went to mentor at Jason's school. Noticing that Jason kept much to himself, Larry befriended him. After several weeks of mentoring, Larry learnt that Jason lives with his mom, her boy friend and little sister in a one-bedroom apartment not far from school. Acting on his suspicion that Jason may be suffering from neglect, Larry phoned Jason's mom for permission to take Jason out on weekends. She gladly consented but a few weeks thereafter terminated the mentoring relationship. Larry wrote:

> After taking Jason out on two consecutive Saturdays, to spend time with me, I found out that his father was in prison and that his mother's current boy friend was his sister's father. Jason also told me that he sleeps on the sofa outside the bedroom and that he does most things for himself. Many times when he would run off and play, his mother would hardly notice that he is not home. Once he said he went home after ten o'clock and found his mother having "a good time with her boy friend and his friends." No one asked where he was nor if he had eaten. From what I understand his mother is always having "parties." I felt so sorry for Jason, I promised to pick him up every Saturday. After that, I picked him up a few more times. Then, last Saturday when I went to pick him up he was sitting on the steps with his hands folded on his knees and his head resting on them. When I touched him, I could see that he was crying so I asked him what was wrong. He told me that his mother said that I should not "come around the house anymore." When I asked him if I should talk to his mother, he said no and that if I did he would be

> whipped "whupped." He then put his head down in his arms and never looked back up at me even though I tried to get him to talk… At the school Jason's teacher assigned me another mentee because Jason's mother called to say that her son does not need a mentor, (Mentor: Larry).

While mentors need to be alert to the consequences of mentoring such as Larry's, they must also be cautious not to allow themselves to be victimized by parents. Many parents willingly give support to the mentoring relationship, but not all are likely to participate in the process. For some, mentoring may be viewed as a way to get someone else to do their children's academic homework, as some mentors observed.

> At first Vicki's mom phoned and asked me to assist Vicki with her math homework, then it was her essay, now it's her reading. Soon a pattern began to develop and I was practically spending all my evening visits assisting Vicki with her homework. I had to politely tell Vicki's mom that if she helps with the reading part, I will help with the Math and essays, (Mentor: Caleen).

> I noticed that as I started to help Davon with his schoolwork, his mother would help less and less. This week she didn't help Davon at all. She told him she was busy and if he could get me to help him. I was not very pleased but I did help Davon. I also told him to inform his mom that I have a job and that if she could help him the evenings I have to work, I will help him the other days… To be honest this was just an excuse because I think parents should help their children with their education, not push it off on someone else. Now both of us are helping Davon… (Mentor: Aaron).

The experiences shared by Caleen and Aaron are not unusual. Mentors must be alert to situations in which parents shift some of their parenting responsibilities on to them. **Mentoring is not the assumption of parenting responsibilities but the provision of assistance and guidance that would enable mentees to develop competency and confidence in their own abilities**. This sometimes necessitates the provision of assistance and guidance to parents, especially in instances where parents are young and lack parenting skills.

THINGS TO REMEMBER

- The involvement of parents/guardians in the mentoring process is crucial for the achievement of successful outcomes.
- The non-involvement of parents/guardians is most likely to generate disinterestedness, indifference, conflict and sometimes outright hostility between parents and their mentored children, mentors and mentees, or parents and mentors – all of which hinder progress and successful outcomes.

DISCUSSION QUESTIONS AND EXERCISES

1. Explain why it is crucial for parents/grandparents to support the mentoring effort and outline the approach you would take in involving parents in the process.

2. What are some of the consequences of excluding parents from the mentoring process? Explain.

3. Anika explained what she did when she found out that her mentee's may have harbored some jealousy toward her: What would you have done if you were placed under such circumstances?

4. In your opinion, could Larry have saved his mentoring relationship with Jason? Explain.

5. Outline how you would approach your mentee's parent if you find that she is gradually transferring some of her parenting responsibilities on to you.

CHAPTER 17

Mentors Lack of Understanding of the Community and Neighborhood in Which Mentees Reside Could Undermine the Mentoring Efforts.

Low Income Communities:

In undertaking the task of mentoring, mentors should not overlook or underplay the significance of the community's influence on the lives, behaviors, and perceptions of mentees. Mentees' community and neighborhood greatly influence their life chances. Coming from a low income, socially isolated community with deteriorating neighborhoods, place many mentees at greater risk of failure than those who are not from such backgrounds. *Communities in general, and low income communities in particular, are varied and should not be viewed as homogeneous constellations of poor families with like characteristics.* It is true that low-income communities share a number of common characteristics such as, residents' persistent poverty, economically depressed neighborhoods and deteriorated buildings. All, however, are not alike. Quite often, they vary in terms of their location, infrastructure, residents' composition, common interactive green space, access to transportation, and proximity to public facilities such as schools, playgrounds and health clinics etc., all of which interconnect to influence and impact the quality of life.

Perceptions of Low Income Communities:

Because of their socio-political histories, their residents' socio-economic status, and often their physical location within economically depressed environments, low income communities are viewed as drug infested, crime ridden havens, with dilapidated structures that are unfit for human habitation. So pervasive is this view that it has permeated the minds of many individuals who serve as mentors to at-risk youths. As a result, these mentors have concentrated on providing mentoring services primarily in schools and centers situated away from the lived realities of their mentees. Recognizing that this practice of mentoring is more common among non-African American mentors, one African American mentor remarked:

> "I know all mentors mean well, but can they grasp the harsh conditions these kids have to deal with every day of their lives. Can they really understand what the African American child goes home to after school?... You may have some idea of where the poor child lives, but have you ever been in his environment and walked in his shoes to understand the impact on his young life,... to understand why he is not learning, why he is not behaving...? You don't have to live there to know, you only have to visit from time to time to get the picture, (Mentor: Morris).

Morris' comment finds support in Graue (1998:8) who noted that: "Children cannot possibly remain untouched by their contexts. Just as their contexts are shaped by their presence, children and their contexts mutually constitute each other. To try to think about children without considering their life situations is to strip children and their actions of meaning."

Mentoring and the Communal Context:

At-risk African American youths are not immune to their context of poverty, which often serves to shorten their childhood and undermine their spirit of trust in adults. As Grauve and Walsh (1998: 8) explain:

> A *context is a culturally and historically situated place and time, a specific here and now...*
> Children cannot possibly remain untouched by their contexts. Just as their contexts are shaped by their presence, children and their contexts mutually constitute each other. To try to think about children without considering their life situations is to strip children and their actions of meaning.

Given the social-cultural and economic contexts out of which the majority of at risk youths emerge, many African American mentors, who themselves are from low income neighborhoods, often express doubts regarding the effectiveness of mentors who do not have a good grasp of their mentees' living conditions, or an adequate understanding of mentees' communities.

Lacking in awareness and understanding of the mentees' actual lived circumstances; mentors regularly turn to their own lived conditions as points of references. *If the lived circumstances of the mentors and mentees parallel each other, the shared information could benefit the mentee. If, however, they diverge, they are likely to strain the mentoring relationships.* The following explanation by one mentor will help to shed light on this issue.

> I had a mentor when I was in school. He was not Black but he was a very kind and patient man. He tried very hard to teach me to read and work on math problems. I know he did because I used to see him nearly every other day, but I never took to him... He never seemed to understand where I was coming from... Whenever I left him, I know the conditions I was going home to, a dark room and a refrigerator with little in it. Do you think I would have math and reading on my mind? Oh no! My mind would go blank as soon as I left him to go home...
> After some months, I had another mentor, he too was white but he knew the "hood". I used to see him coaching ball... He took an interest in me and helped me with school. When we talked, you know he understood. It's like he knew me and some of my "boys" [friends] inside out... He knew we were sometimes hungry. He even took us to McDonalds... He has a lot to do with me coming to college today (Mentor: Kelvin).

We see from the above example that a mentor's race does not restrict him from obtaining a first hand look, which helps in acquiring a better understanding of the mentee's residential community. It is true that non-African Americans are seldom socialized to develop a "double consciousness" in Du Boisian sense of the term. Over time, however, many do develop an understanding of the plight of African Americans based on their interactions and active participation within the African American community. And, while the visible difference in their race may often be perceived as a draw back, it has not deterred many non-African Americans from visiting and assisting mentees within the confines of the mentees residential community settings.

Sometimes, a hindrance in the mentoring process is not the mentors' race but their social class backgrounds. More readily than race, however, class barriers begin to fade as mentors develop a better understanding of their mentees and the low-income neighborhoods in which they reside. What seems to account for initial apprehensions about mentoring at-risk youths are the conflicting views shared by middle class African Americans regarding low income families. As a middle class gentleman said to me in reference to one of the communities where my students and I mentor, “I wouldn’t go there. That place is full of dope dealers, vagrants and people who don’t know what to do with their lives.”

THINGS TO REMEMBER

- Low income communities are varied and should not be viewed as a homogeneous constellation of single-parent-welfare mothers.
- The communities in which mentees live influence and impact their lives.
- Because of the negative social forces so prevalent in low income communities –drugs, crime, violence, prostitution, absence of recreational facilities, etc. – these often serve to warp mentees perceptions of reality, shorten their childhood and help undermine their trust in adults and hopes for success.
- A lack of awareness of mentees’ communities and their lived circumstances regularly contributes to false notions regarding the expectations, methods and effectiveness of mentoring.

DISCUSSION QUESTIONS AND EXERCISES

1. Discuss the ways in which low-income communities place youths at-risk?

2. At-risk African American youths are not immune to their context of poverty, which often serves to shorten their childhood and undermine their spirit of trust in adults: Explain whether you agree or disagree with this statement.

3. Visit your mentee's neighborhood and write a detailed description of it. Describe how you feel about the neighborhood, and then compare this with the descriptions and feelings provided by your mentee. Use this information to regularly refine your mentoring strategy.

Appendix

The information in this monograph is based on documented observations of and discussions with over three hundred Florida Agricultural and Mechanical University (FAMU) students and the author, all of whom served as mentors from Spring 1996 to Fall 2003. Assigned to mentees, students received classroom instructions and training on the social problems of youth, mentoring, anger management and observational research, thereby enabling them to serve the dual functions of mentors and ethnographic observers.

Mentees came primarily from the Leon county school system with a few from neighboring Gadsen county. These were students whom the school system identified to be at-risk. Other mentees came to us by way of parents and/or grandparents requests. Some of these were already entangled within the juvenile justice system. Mentees ranged from age six through seventeen, and resided various low income communities throughout the county.

Under my supervision, mentors met with their mentees in the school and community settings at a minimum of once per week to observe classroom conduct and serve as tutors. Mentors also visited their mentees' homes, and occasionally took mentees' out to shopping malls, cinemas, their homes, and to organized games and sporting events. On several occasions, the mentors and the author had to accompany parents and mentees to court and other government agencies in efforts to assist them with their problems.

As a way to identify mentees' problems and assist with their behavioral conduct and academic performance, mentors maintained journals in which they recorded their observations, feelings and interactions with their mentees. Mentors journals, along with the mentoring experience became the focus of classroom discussions, and problem solving sessions. During the first year of mentoring, mentors were not required to maintain journals. This led to the quick discovery that many mentors failed to capture the subtleties of their mentees' behaviors, as well as their responses and reflections on the mentoring activity.

The information presented in this monograph is drawn from mentors' journals, classroom discussions on the mentoring experience, the author's mentoring, observations and visits with mentors to the schools and surrounding communities, visits to juvenile court in Leon and Gadsen counties, as well as individual and group meetings with parents and grandparents. In drawing from the mentoring experience, the contents of mentors' journals were reviewed to identify repeatable concepts and themes. These concepts and themes were then grouped and carefully analyzed across mentoring reports and discussion notes to assess the veracity of the field data collected and presented over the years. After grouping and regrouping the concepts and themes, following in part Glaser and Strauss' grounded theory approach, some definitive statements began to emerge. These statements were then used to formulate lessons learned from the mentoring experience.

REFERENCES

Anderson, L. P. (1999). Parentification in the Context of the African American Family. In Chase (Ed.), *Burdened Children* (154-170). Thousand Oaks, California: Sage publications.

Arrigo, B. A. (1999). *Social Justice, Criminal Justice.* Canada: Wadsworth Publishing Company.

Barras, J. (2000). *Whatever Happened to Daddy's Little Girl: The Impact of Fatherlessness on Black Women.* New York: Ballantine Publishing Group.

Barsky, A. E. (2000). *Conflict Resolution for the Helping Professions.* Canada: Wadsworth.

Bartollas, C. & Miller, S. J. (1994). *Juvenile Justice in America (3rd Ed.).* Upper Saddle River, New Jersey: Prentice Hall.

Billingsley, A. (1968). *Black Families in White America.* Englewood Cliffs, N.J: Prentice Hall.

Blackwell, J. E. (1991). *The Black Community: Diversity and Unity.* NY: Harper Collins Publishers Inc.

Blechman, E. A. (1992). Mentors for High-Risk Minority Youth: From Effective Communication to Bicultural Competence. *Journal of Clinical Child Psychology*, 21(2) 16-69.

Boyd, H. & Allen, R. L. (Ed.). (1996). *Brotherman: The odyssey of Black men in America – An Anthology.* New York: Ballantine Books.

CampbellJones, B. & CampbellJones, F. (2003). Educating African American Children: Credibility at a Crossroads. In Schultz, F. (Ed.), *Multicultural Education 03/04*, (142-147). Guilford, CT: McGraw Hill/Dushkin.

Coles, R. (1993). Mentoring. In *The Call of Service: A Witness to Idealsim.* Boston: Houghton Mifflin.

Collins, P. H. (1999). The meaning of Motherhood in Black Culture. In Robert Staples (Ed.), *The Black Family* (157-166). Canada: Wadsworth Publishing Company.

Comer, J. P. (2003). Schools That Develop Children. In Finsterbusch, K. (Ed.), *Sociology 03/04*, (148- 53). Guilford, CT: McGraw Hill/Dushkin.

Dubois, W. E. (1961). *The Souls of Black Folk.* New York: Fawcett Publications, Inc.

Feagin, J. R. (1989). *Racial and Ethnic Relations.* Englewood Cliffs, New Jersey: Prentice Hall.

Ferrara, F. (2002). *Childhood Sexual Abuse*. Canada, Thomson Learning.

Franklin II, C. W. (1999). Sex and Class Differences in the Socialization Experiences of African American Youth. In Robert Staples (Ed.), *The Black Family* (248-257). Canada: Wadsworth Publishing Company.

Garbarino, J. (1999). *Lost Boys: Why Our Sons Turn Violent and How We Can Save Them.* New York: Anchor Books.

Glaser, B. G. & Strauss, A. L. (1967). *The Discovery of Grounded theory: Strategies for Qualitative Research.* New York: Aldine Publishing Company.

Graue, M. E. & Walsh, D. J. (1998). *Studying Children in Context; Theories, Methods, and Ethics.* Thousand Oaks, California: Sage Publications.

Hamer, J. (2001). *What it means to be Daddy: Fatherhood for Black Men Living Away from Their Children*. New York: Columbia University Press.

Harris, S. M. (1999). Black Male Masculinity and Same Sex Friendships. In Robert Staples (Ed.), *The Black Family* (77-85). Canada: Wadsworth Publishing Company.

Harris, Y. R., Terrel, D. & Allen, G. (1999). The Influence of Education Context and Beliefs on the Teaching Behavior of African American Mothers. *Journal of Black Psychology,* 25(4) 490-503.

Hartmann, T. (1998). *Healing ADD.* Grass Valley, CA: Underwood Books.

Hill, S. A. (1999). *African American Children: Socialization and Development in Families.* Thousand Oaks, CA: Sage Publications.

Horn, W. F. (1999). The Absence of Fathers Puts teens At Risk. In Egendorf, L. K. & Hurley, J. A. *Teens at Risk: Opposing Viewpoints* (38 – 51). San Diego, California: Green Haven Press, Inc.

Hrabowski III, A. F., Maton, I. K. & Grief, G. L. (1998). *Beating the Odds: Raising Successful African American Males.* New York: Oxford University Press.

Jewell, K. S. (1988). *Survival of the Black Family.* New York: Praeger.

Kendall, D. (1997). *Race, Class and Gender In A Diverse Society.* Needham Heights. Allyn and Bacon.

Kitwana, B. (2002). *The Hip Hop Generation.* NY: Basic Citivas Books.

Knowles, L. L. & Prewitt, K. (2001). Institutional and Ideological Roots of racism. In A. Aguirre and D. Baker (Ed.), *Race and Ethnicity* (3rd Ed.) 48-57.
Kozol, J. (2000). *Ordinary Resurrections*: Children in the Years of Hope. NY:Perennial.

Kronick, R. F. (1999). When a Professor Learns from Students: Dilemmas Derived from "At Risk Youth." *Journal of Offender Rehabilitation*, 28(3/4) 135-143.

Kunjufu, J. (2002). *Black Students – Middle Class Teachers.* Chicago, Illinois: African American Images.

Lempert, L. B. (1999). Other Fathers: An Alternative Perspective on African American Community Caring. In Staples (Ed.). *The Black Family* (189 – 201). Canada: Wadsworth Publishing Company.

Lum, D. (Ed.) (2003). *Culturally Competent Practice (2nd. Ed.)* Canada: Brooks/Cole.

Mackey, C. W. (1997). Single-Parent Families Contribute to Violent Crime. In Karen L. Swisher (Ed.), *Single Parent Families* (53-59). San Diego, CA: Green Haven Press.

Maginnis, L. R. (1997). Single-Parent Families Cause Juvenile Crime. In A. E. Sadler (Ed.), *Juvenile Crime: Opposing Viewpoints* (62-66). San Diego, CA: Green Haven Press, Inc.

Majors, R.., & Billson, J. M. (1992). *Cool Pose: The Dilemmas of Black Manhood in America.* New York: Touchstone.

McAdoo, H. P. (1982). Black Mothers and the Extended Family Support Network. In La Frances Rodgers-Rose, (Ed.), *The Black Woman* (154-158). Beverly Hills California: Sage Publications.

McAdoo, H. P. (2002). The Village Talks: Racial Socialization of Our Children. In Harriette P. McAdoo (Ed.), *Black Children* (2nd Ed.), (47-55). Thousand Oaks, CA: Sage Publications.

McCall, N. (1994). Makes Me Wanna Holler. New York: Random House.

McLanahan, S. (1994). The Consequences of Single Motherhood. American Prospect (Summer).

McRoy, G. R. (2003). Cultural Competence with African Americans. In Lum, D. (Ed.). *Culturally Competent Practice* (217 – 237). Canada: Brooks/Cole.

McWhirter, J. J., McWhirter, B. T., McWhirter, A. M., & McWhirter, E. H. (1998). *At-Risk Youth* (2nd Ed.). USA: Brooks/Cole Publishing Company.

McWright, L. (2002). African American geandmothers' and grandfathers' Influence in the Value Socialization of Grandchildren. In Harriet P. McAdoo (Ed.), Black Children (27-44). Thousand Oaks, California: Sage Publications.

Mech, E. V., Pryde, J. A. & Rycraft, J.R. (1995). Mentors for Adolescents in Foster Care. *Child and Adolescent Social Work Journal*, 12(4) 317-328.

Mills, C. W. (2000). *The Sociological Imagination.* New York: Oxford University Press.

Moynihan, D. P. (1999). The Negro Family. In Staples, R. (Ed.). *The Black Family* (7 – 17). Canada: Wadsworth Publishing Company.

Ogawa, B. K. (1999). *Color of Justice: Culturally Sensitive treatment of Minority Crime Victims* (2nd Ed.). Boston: Allyn and Bacon.

Palmer, C. A. (1998). Passageways: *An Interpretive History of Black America, Volume 1: 1619 – 1863.* New York: Holt, Rinehart and Winston.

Parks, G. (1963). *The Learning Tree.* New York: Ballantine Books.

Popenoe, D. (1996). *Life Without Father.* New York: the Free Press.

Rivers, S. W. & Rivers, F. (2002). Sankofa Shule Spells Success for African American Children. In Harriette P. McAdoo (Ed.), *Black Children* (2nd Ed.), (175-189). Thousand Oaks, CA: Sage Publications.

Scott, J. W. (1999). African-American Daughter-Mother Relations and Teenage Pregnancy: Two Faces of Premarital Teenage Pregnancy. In Staples (Ed.). *The Black Family* (167 – 178). Canada: Wadsworth Publishing Company.

See, L. A., Bowles, D. & Darlington, M. (1998). Young African American grandmothers: A Missed Developmental Stage. In L. A. See (Ed.). *Human Behavior in the Social Environment from an African American Perspective* (281-301). New York: the Haworth Press, Inc.

Shusta, R. M., Levine, D. R., Harris, P. R. & Wong, H. Z. (1995). *Multicultural Law Enforcement: Strategies for Peacekeeping in a Diverse Society.* Upper Saddle River, New Jersey: Prentice Hall.

Staples, R. (1999). In a Community of Women. In Robert Staples (Ed.), *The Black Family* (67-69). Canada: Wadsworth Publishing Company.

Staples, R. (1999). Social Cultural Factors in Black Family Transformation: Toward a redefinition of Family Functions. In Staples (Ed.). *The Black Family* (18 – 23). Canada: Wadsworth Publishing Company.

Staples, R. (1999). The Dyad. In Robert Staples (Ed.), *The Black Family* (40-44). Canada: Wadsworth Publishing Company.

Staples, R. (1999). The Family. In Robert Staples (Ed.), *The Black Family* (152-155). Canada: Wadsworth Publishing Company.

Stephens, R. D. & Arnette, J. L. (February 2000). *From the Courthouse to the Schoolhouse: Making Successful Transitions.* Washington, DC: Office of Juvenile justice and Delinquency Prevention.

Suskind, R. (1998). *A Hope in the UNSEEN.* New York: Broadway Books.
Taylor, M. & Stephenson, J. (1996). What is Mentoring? In Mick Mawer (Ed.), *Mentoring in Physical Education: Issues and Insights,* (22-38). London: The Falmer Press.

U.S. Department of Justice, Office of Juvenile Justice and Delinquency Prevention. (1996, March). *Combating Violence and Delinquency: The National Juvenile Justice Action Plan.* Washington, DC: U.S. Department of Justice.

Upchurch, C. (1997). *Convicted in the Womb.* New York: Bantam Books.

Walker, G. & Freedman, M. (1996). Social Change One on One: The New Mentoring Movement. *The American Prospect*, July/August, 75-81.

Whitehead, D. B. (1997). Single-Parent Families Are harmful. In Karen L. Swisher (Ed.), *Single Parent Families* (10-40). San Diego, CA: Green Haven Press.

Wickman, F. & Sjodin, T. (1997). *Mentoring: The Most Obvious Yet Overlooked Key to Achieving More in Life than You Dreamed Possible.* Chicago: Irwin Professional Publishing.

Wilson, J. (1996). *When Work Disappears.* New York: Vintage Books.

Yoest, C. C. (1996). Fount of Virtue, Spring of Wealth: How the Strong Family Sustains a Prosperous Society. In Harold A. Widdison (Ed.), *Social problems 96-97*, (23-34). Guilford, CT: Dushkin Publishing Group.